RICH THROUGH HIS POVERTY

Michael E.B. Maher

Unless otherwise indicated, all Scripture quotations in this teaching are from the *New King James Version* of the bible.

2018

ISBN: 978-0-6399432-0-6

Books by Michael E.B. Maher

Repentance from Dead Works
Faith Toward God
Doctrine of Baptisms
Laying on of Hands
Resurrection of the Dead
Eternal Judgement
Born Free from Sin
The Will of Man
The Conscience of Man
The Spirit of Man
The Mind of Man
The Body of Man
Spiritual Gifts
The Revelation Gifts
The Power Gifts
The Speaking Gifts
Ministry Gifts
There is Sin to Death
Prayer
Being led by the Spirit
Overcoming Unforgiveness
The Two Gospels Explained
Of Such is the Kingdom
The Last Days

For my wife Patricia

Contents

Chapter 1 1
It is God's will that we prosper 1
God is able 1
God is willing 11
Chapter 2 17
God's view of prosperity 17
The servants and children of God 17
What does it mean to be rich? 19
Contentment versus covetousness 24
Chapter 3 29
New testament examples 29
Jesus' early years 29
Jesus' home 34
Jesus' generosity 36
Jesus' ministry finances 40
Jesus' personal finances 44
The Lord's ministers 48
The Lord's saints 57
Chapter 4 65
Walking in prosperity 65
The gospel to the poor 65
Faith requires action 70
A balanced lifestyle 72

Giving	77
Tithing	84
Creating wealth	91
Divine favour	94
Chapter 5	95
Our adversary	95
There is only one thief	95
Our hedge	96
Our authority	99

Chapter 1
It is God's will that we prosper

There is much controversy in the church today, about the "prosperity gospel". There are those who promote it to the extreme, and there are those who are against it in its entirety. Each side tends to accuse the other, of teaching error. As with most doctrines in the bible, where there are two opposing views taught, invariably the truth of God's word, is found somewhere in the middle. This book examines just what God's word says on the subject of prosperity, particularly for those under the new covenant, for that is the covenant that we partake of.

God is able

Matthew 6:24-33 "No one can serve two masters; for either he will hate the one and love the other, or else he will be loyal to the one and despise the other. You cannot serve God and mammon. (25) "Therefore, I say to you, do not worry about your life, what you will eat or what you will drink; nor about your body, what you will put on. Is not life more than food and the body more than clothing? (26) Look at the birds of the air, for they neither sow nor reap nor gather into barns; yet your heavenly Father feeds them. Are you not of more value than they? (27) Which of you by worrying can add one cubit to his stature? (28) "So why do you worry about clothing? Consider the lilies of the field, how

It is God's will that we prosper

they grow: they neither toil nor spin; (29) and yet I say to you that even Solomon in all his glory was not arrayed like one of these. (30) Now if God so clothes the grass of the field, which today is, and tomorrow is thrown into the oven, will He not much more clothe you, O you of little faith? (31) "Therefore, do not worry, saying, 'What shall we eat?' or 'What shall we drink?' or 'What shall we wear?' (32) For after all these things the Gentiles seek. For your heavenly Father knows that you need all these things. (33) But seek first the kingdom of God and His righteousness, and all these things shall be added to you."

There can be no doubt, that in the above passage of scripture, our Lord Jesus was teaching us how God our Father, is well able to take care of all our physical needs, in this life. In teaching us the truth about God supplying all our needs, our Lord assures us that God knows our every need, and that He is more than able, to supply each one of those needs. For as God takes care of His entire creation, so He is well able, to take care of the needs, of each one of His children. And so, for us to doubt God's ability to supply our needs, is to doubt His ability to take care of His creation, which is foolishness, for we see evidence all around us every day, of just how God does take care of His entire creation. In this chapter, we are discussing the truth as revealed in the new testament, that it is God's will for His children to prosper. There are many areas of our lives that God wants us to prosper in, including our spiritual growth, but in this book, we are specifically dealing with the area of finances.

It is God's will that we prosper

2 Corinthians 9:8 "And God is able to make all grace abound toward you, that you, always having all sufficiency in all things, may have an abundance for every good work."

The context of the above passage of scripture, deals specifically with the area of finances. And in this passage, the Holy Spirit through the apostle Paul, tells us that God is able to make all grace abound toward us, so that we will always have more than we need, and will therefore, always be able to help others who are in need. So, with regards the area of finances, just what does the Holy Spirit mean, when He says that God is able to make all grace abound toward us? One of the ways in which God makes His grace abound towards us, in the area of finances, is that He gives us favour, with those who are in a position to bless us financially. For example, if we work for an employer, God is able to give us favour with our employer, so that we will receive above average increases in our salaries, and also, promotions in our place of work.

Genesis 39:1-4 "Now Joseph had been taken down to Egypt. And Potiphar, an officer of Pharaoh, captain of the guard, an Egyptian, bought him from the Ishmaelites who had taken him down there. (2) The Lord was with Joseph, and he was a successful man; and he was in the house of his master the Egyptian. (3) And his master saw that the Lord was with him and that the Lord made all he did to prosper in his hand. (4) So, Joseph found favour in his sight, and served him. Then he made him overseer of his house, and all that he had he put under his authority."

It is God's will that we prosper

The above passage of scripture, is an example of just how the Lord gives us favour, with those for whom we work. Although in this example, Joseph was a slave to his master, the principle remains the same with regards to any employer, employee relationship. God gave Joseph favour with Potiphar, who was in a position to bless him, and so Potiphar promoted Joseph to become the overseer of his entire estate. Obviously, Joseph was diligent as a slave, and so God could use that to give him favour in Potiphar's eyes, but I don't want to discuss that aspect in this chapter, for all I want to establish in this section, is that God is able to make all grace abound toward us, and what that means.

Exodus 2:15-21 "When Pharaoh heard of this matter, he sought to kill Moses. But Moses fled from the face of Pharaoh and dwelt in the land of Midian; and he sat down by a well. (16) Now the priest of Midian had seven daughters. And they came and drew water, and they filled the troughs to water their father's flock. (17) Then the shepherds came and drove them away; but Moses stood up and helped them and watered their flock. (18) When they came to Reuel their father, he said, "How is it that you have come so soon today?" (19) And they said, "An Egyptian delivered us from the hand of the shepherds, and he also drew enough water for us and watered the flock." (20) So, he said to his daughters, "And, where is he? Why is it that you have left the man? Call him, that he may eat bread." (21) Then Moses was content to live with the man, and he gave Zipporah his daughter to Moses."

It is God's will that we prosper

So, what about those who are unemployed, and are looking for employment? In these instances, God is able to give us favour with those who are able to employ us, so that we will have employment. In the above account in scripture, we see Moses unemployed, at forty years of age. He had been raised in Pharaoh's household as the son of Pharaoh's daughter, but at the age of forty, God had impressed upon Moses that He was going to use Moses, to deliver the children of Israel. Moses missed God's leading, by thinking that God was going to use him in his capacity as a ruler in Egypt, to bring about Israel's deliverance, and so he tried to bring about their deliverance in his own strength. That went horribly wrong for him, and he had to flee Egypt as a result. And so, at forty years of age, Moses ended up in the land of Midian, unemployed. But even though Moses was himself in dire straits, he still gave assistance to those in need, where he could. And in this account, Moses helped the daughters of Reuel, the priest of Midian. Moses was not looking for any recompense for that which he did, and he had no idea of the ramifications of his actions. But nevertheless, God was able to use his actions, to give him favour with Reuel, who then offered Moses employment. Over time, Moses proved to be such a good employee, that he eventually married the boss's daughter.

Genesis 30:30-34 "For what you had before I came was little, and it has increased to a great amount; the Lord has blessed you since my coming. And now, when shall I also provide for my own house?" (31) So, he said, "What shall I give you?" And Jacob said, "You shall not give me anything. If you will do this thing for me, I will again feed and keep your flocks: (32) Let me pass through all your

It is God's will that we prosper

flock today, removing from there all the speckled and spotted sheep, and all the brown ones among the lambs, and the spotted and speckled among the goats; and these shall be my wages. (33) So, my righteousness will answer for me in time to come, when the subject of my wages comes before you: every one that is not speckled and spotted among the goats, and brown among the lambs, will be considered stolen, if it is with me." (34) And Laban said, "Oh, that it were according to your word!"

So, what about those who are themselves employers, i.e. those who own their own businesses? In these instances, God is able to give us favour with those who are able to assist us with the capital we need, to start and grow our businesses. In the above passage of scripture, we see the account of the start-up, of Jacob's own business. Up until this time, Jacob had been working for Laban as an employee, and God had blessed Laban, because Jacob worked for him. And so, Jacob now wanted to start his own business, and he made a business proposal to Laban. Because God gave Jacob favour with Laban, he readily agreed to Jacob's proposal. The essence of Jacob's proposal, was that he would remove all the speckled, and spotted, and brown, goats and sheep, from Laban's herds, and it was those that Jacob would use as start-up capital for his own business. Obviously, there were very few speckled, and spotted, and brown, goats and sheep, in Laban's flocks at the time, which is why he was so eager to agree to Jacob's proposal. Nevertheless, God had given Jacob favour with Laban, who in turn supplied Jacob with the start-up capital he needed, to start his own business.

It is God's will that we prosper

Genesis 30:40-43 "Then Jacob separated the lambs and made the flocks face toward the streaked and all the brown in the flock of Laban; but he put his own flocks by themselves and did not put them with Laban's flock. (41) And it came to pass, whenever the stronger livestock conceived, that Jacob placed the rods before the eyes of the livestock in the gutters, that they might conceive among the rods. (42) But when the flocks were feeble, he did not put them in; so, the feebler were Laban's and the stronger Jacob's. (43) Thus, the man became exceedingly prosperous, and had large flocks, female and male servants, and camels and donkeys."

Genesis 31:10-12 "And it happened, at the time when the flocks conceived, that I lifted my eyes and saw in a dream, and behold, the rams which leaped upon the flocks were streaked, speckled, and gray-spotted. (11) Then the Angel of God spoke to me in a dream, saying, 'Jacob.' And I said, 'Here I am.' (12) And He said, 'Lift your eyes now and see, all the rams which leap on the flocks are streaked, speckled, and gray-spotted; for I have seen all that Laban is doing to you."

There is another aspect, to the way that God makes His grace abound toward us in the area of finances, and that is in the area of creative ideas that He gives us. In the first passage of scripture quoted above, we see the business practice that Jacob implemented to grow his business. And as a result of Jacob implementing that business idea, he grew his business from the start-up capital that Laban had given him, into a business that made him exceedingly prosperous. It is in the second

It is God's will that we prosper

passage of scripture quoted however, that God reveals to us, where Jacob received his idea for his business to succeed. God had given Jacob his idea in a dream, and as a result of Jacob implementing that idea, God enabled his business to grow, through which he became exceedingly prosperous.

> *Genesis 24:35 "The Lord has blessed my master greatly, and he has become great; and He has given him flocks and herds, silver and gold, male and female servants, and camels and donkeys."*

For those of us who already have businesses that are in operation, God is able to make all grace abound toward us, in our businesses. What that means, is that God is able to give us favour in the marketplace, so that our businesses will continue to grow and prosper. In the above passage of scripture, Abraham's chief steward, was relating to Laban and Bethuel, just how much God had prospered Abraham's business over the years.

> *Job 42:10-12 "And the Lord restored Job's losses when he prayed for his friends. Indeed, the Lord gave Job twice as much as he had before. (11) Then all his brothers, all his sisters, and all those who had been his acquaintances before, came to him and ate food with him in his house; and they consoled him and comforted him for all the adversity that the Lord had brought upon him. Each one gave him a piece of silver and each a ring of gold. (12) Now the Lord blessed the latter days of Job more than his beginning; for he had fourteen thousand sheep, six thousand camels, one thousand yoke of oxen, and one thousand female donkeys."*

It is God's will that we prosper

It is not uncommon in the body of Christ, for one at some point in their walk with the Lord, to lose everything that they have. I am not referring to those who voluntarily give up all for the kingdom of God, as they follow the Lord in the calling that He places upon their lives. I am referring to those who lose everything, as a result of external factors impacting on their lives, and not as a result of their own actions. We do not always understand the reasons for this happening, only the Lord does. In the above passage of scripture, we have the account of when Job lost everything, and at the end of his ordeal, God caused everyone that Job knew, to take up a collection for him, which resulted in Job having sufficient start-up capital to start a new business, that God blessed abundantly, so much so, that God restored all of Job's loses, and in fact God gave him twice as much as he had before.

2 Kings 4:1-7 "A certain woman of the wives of the sons of the prophets cried out to Elisha, saying, "Your servant my husband is dead, and you know that your servant feared the Lord. And the creditor is coming to take my two sons to be his slaves." (2) So, Elisha said to her, "What shall I do for you? Tell me, what do you have in the house?" And she said, "Your maidservant has nothing in the house but a jar of oil." (3) Then he said, "Go, borrow vessels from everywhere, from all your neighbours--empty vessels; do not gather just a few. (4) And when you have come in, you shall shut the door behind you and your sons; then pour it into all those vessels and set aside the full ones." (5) So, she went from him and shut the door behind her and her sons, who brought

It is God's will that we prosper

the vessels to her; and she poured it out. (6) Now it came to pass, when the vessels were full, that she said to her son, "Bring me another vessel." And he said to her, "There is not another vessel." So, the oil ceased. (7) Then she came and told the man of God. And he said, "Go, sell the oil and pay your debt; and you and your sons live on the rest."

All of the examples that we have looked at in this section so far, of how God blessed His saints financially, are supernatural, for it was God who caused the individuals to be blessed. But although all the examples were supernatural, not all were spectacular. The above account in scripture, is an example how God can also bless His saints in not only a supernatural way, but also in a spectacular way. The context of the above passage, is that one of the prophets that worked with Elisha, had passed away, and he had left his wife and sons without any means of support, and a large amount of debt. The prophet's wife had come to Elisha to ask him to assist them, and so God worked a spectacular miracle through His prophet Elisha. For God multiplied the oil she had, to the point that she was able to pay off all her debt, and live off the balance of the proceeds, for the rest of her life. Although this example, is not the normal way in which God supplies our needs, nevertheless He is well able to do spectacular miracles, when the need arises. And so, in this section, I have endeavoured to list the most common financial scenarios, that can occur in our lives. And in each scenario, I have given a biblical example, of how God blessed His saints financially, and caused them to prosper. Although I have only given one example in each case, there are many other accounts in scripture, that could be quoted in each case, to support the truth that

It is God's will that we prosper

God is able to bless us, no matter what financial condition we may find ourselves in. And so, through the above examples, and the passages of scripture quoted earlier, we can clearly see that God is more than able, to make all grace abound toward us, so that not only are all of our needs met, but we will also have more than enough, so that we can help others who are themselves in need.

God is willing

Matthew 6:31-33 "Therefore do not worry, saying, 'What shall we eat?' or 'What shall we drink?' or 'What shall we wear?' (32) For after all these things the Gentiles seek. For your heavenly Father knows that you need all these things. (33) But seek first the kingdom of God and His righteousness, and all these things shall be added to you."

We have seen in the previous section, that God is well able to make all grace abound toward us, so that all of our needs are met, and more. Nevertheless, while most believers will agree, that God is able to make all grace abound toward us in the area of finances, not all agree, that God is willing to do so. But if we go back to the words of our Lord Jesus as quoted above, we see very clearly that God our Father, is very willing to supply all of our needs, for Jesus says that everything we need, will be added to us. According to Jesus, the only condition that needs to be met in order for God to supply our needs, is that we need to be a part of His family, and all believers meet that condition. Think about that in the natural. If we had an earthly father, who not only knew what our needs were, but also had an abundance of resources available to meet

It is God's will that we prosper

those needs, would he not freely take care of those needs? Indeed, we would consider that a father in such a position, who refused to supply his children's needs, was a wicked parent. In fact, the scripture teaches us, that a father that refuses to provide for his own household, has denied the faith and is worse than an unbeliever (1 Timothy 5:8). God our Father is not a hypocrite. He would not instruct us as earthly fathers, to provide for the needs of our children, and then Himself not do the same for His children. When you think about it in that light, then it becomes an insult to God, to not believe that He is more than willing to supply all of our needs.

2 Corinthians 8:9 "For you know the grace of our Lord Jesus Christ, that though He was rich, yet for your sakes He became poor, that you through His poverty might become rich."

The above passage of scripture, also clearly reveals to us, that it is the will of God, for His children to prosper. The context of this passage, is dealing with the financial wellbeing of the saints, in this life, and we need to interpret this scripture in that light. Obviously, this scripture also refers to our eternal rewards in heaven. Nevertheless, when you read the context of this passage, very clearly, the Holy Spirit is referring to our financial needs, in this life. And so, we see that our Lord Jesus, has made provision for us to become rich, in this life. He did so, by making Himself poor, so that through His poverty, we may become rich. If it was not the will of God for us to become rich, then Jesus would not have done what He did. You will recall that our Lord Jesus stated at one time, "Go and tell John the things you have seen and heard: that the blind see, the lame walk, the lepers are cleansed,

It is God's will that we prosper

the deaf hear, the dead are raised, the poor have the gospel preached to them" (Luke 7:22). None would dispute, that all the healing miracles, and the miracles of raising the dead, that our Lord did, took place in this life. And so, if that is the case, why would we think that the Lord was not referring to the poor, in this life, also having their physical needs met? Clearly, our Lord preaches the gospel (good news) to the poor, by telling them that God our Father is not only able, but also willing to meet all their needs.

> *Philippians 4:19 "And my God shall supply all your need according to His riches in glory by Christ Jesus."*

Again, in the above passage of scripture, the Holy Spirit through the apostle Paul, reveals to us that God our Father, will supply all of our needs. The context of this passage, also clearly deals with the financial needs of the saints. If God were not willing to meet our needs, then the Holy Spirit would never have allowed the apostle Paul to teach this concept to the saints. This is a promise of God given to us in scripture, and the bible teaches us that all the promises of God, are "yes" and "amen" in Christ Jesus (2 Corinthians 1:20). What that means, is that when we claim that promise from God our Father, because we are in Christ, then God always answers by saying, yes and amen, i.e. yes, so be it done to you My child. Notice that the above scripture does not say that God will supply some of our needs, but rather that God will supply "all" of our needs. In other words, God is not selective as to which needs He will supply, and which needs He will ignore, for He supplies them all. The scripture also tells us that God supplies our needs according to His riches. Our Father's

It is God's will that we prosper

riches are limitless, and so He has no problem meeting every need we may have.

> *3 John 1:2 "Beloved, I pray that you may prosper in all things and be in health, just as your soul prospers."*

The Holy Spirit taught the apostle John, to pray the above prayer, for the saints. John clearly understood and taught us the truth, that God only hears our prayers, if we pray according to His will (1 John 5:14). And so, the apostle John would not have prayed this prayer for the saints, if it were not the express will of God the Father, that His children prosper in all things, and be in health. God is not confused. And so, He would not instruct us to pray for something that is contrary to His will for our lives. And so, you will not find one place in the new testament, where God states that it is not His express will, that His children prosper and walk in health. On the contrary, we have seen a number of scriptures that prove categorically, that it is our Father's express will, that we do prosper, and walk in health.

> *Galatians 3:13-14 "Christ has redeemed us from the curse of the law, having become a curse for us (for it is written, "Cursed is everyone who hangs on a tree"), (14) that the blessing of Abraham might come upon the Gentiles in Christ Jesus, that we might receive the promise of the Spirit through faith."*

Our Lord Jesus Christ did everything for us when He went to the cross. There is nothing that we can do to inherit the promises of God, for Jesus has done it all. One

It is God's will that we prosper

of the things that our Lord did for us, is that He became a curse for us, thus redeeming us from the curse of the law. This truth is revealed to us in the above passage of scripture. So, what is the curse of the law, that our Lord Jesus has redeemed us from? The curse of the law, is recorded in the book of Deuteronomy, chapter twenty-eight. Part of that curse, is financial lack. There can be no doubt that poverty is a curse, and not a blessing, for if it were a blessing, then God would not have listed it under the curse. So, in that light, the above passage of scripture, could just as easily have been written that, "Christ has redeemed us from the curse of poverty, having become poor for us". That ties in with the scripture that we read earlier, where it was stated, that for our sakes, Christ became poor, that we through His poverty, might become rich (2 Corinthians 8:9). Again, if it were not the express will of God our Father, that we as His children should walk free from poverty, and walk in financial blessing, then He would not have allowed His Son to become a curse for us, thus redeeming us from the curse of the law. In this section, we have seen conclusive proof, that it is our Father's express will that, as His children, we walk in financial prosperity. And so, for one to continue to doubt this truth, is to doubt the integrity of God our Father and our Lord Jesus Christ.

It is God's will that we prosper

Chapter 2
God's view of prosperity

The servants and children of God

Deuteronomy 6:10-12 "So it shall be, when the Lord your God brings you into the land of which He swore to your fathers, to Abraham, Isaac, and Jacob, to give you large and beautiful cities which you did not build, (11) houses full of all good things, which you did not fill, hewn-out wells which you did not dig, vineyards and olive trees which you did not plant--when you have eaten and are full-- (12) then beware, lest you forget the Lord who brought you out of the land of Egypt, from the house of bondage."

Under the old covenant, the children of Israel were the Lord's servants and not His children, for they were not born-again (Leviticus 25:55). And yet, as revealed to us in the above passage of scripture, under that covenant, the Lord freely gave to each one of His servants, houses full of all good things, which they had not filled, hewn-out wells which they had not dug, and vineyards and olive trees which they did not plant. In other words, God gave them everything they needed to live comfortable lives, in this life. Under the new covenant, we are children of God, and not His servants, for we are born-again. And so, if God took care of the needs of His servants in this manner under the old covenant, how much more will God take care of the needs of His children under the new covenant, which is a better covenant established upon better promises (Hebrews 8:6). None can dispute that God

God's view of prosperity

provided a home, and a more than adequate means of income, for each of His servants under the old covenant. Therefore, God's children under the new covenant, can expect to receive from Him, at least the same, if not more.

Leviticus 26:2-5 "I am the Lord. (3) 'If you walk in My statutes and keep My commandments, and perform them, (4) then I will give you rain in its season, the land shall yield its produce, and the trees of the field shall yield their fruit. (5) Your threshing shall last till the time of vintage, and the vintage shall last till the time of sowing; you shall eat your bread to the full, and dwell in your land safely."

When God blessed His servants under the old covenant, He did not make all of them multi-millionaires, or even millionaires. No rather, from the above passage of scripture, we can see that God blessed their means of income, which was primarily farming, so that they never experienced any lack, and they always had more than they needed. Now there were among the children of Israel, some who for various reasons, did become very wealthy, but that was not the norm, for God had not promised to make them all wealthy, but He had promised to give them all a full supply. Boaz was an example of one who became very wealthy through godly principles (Ruth 2:1), while Nabal was an example of one who became very rich through ungodly principles (1 Samuel 25:2). And so, we can see from these two examples, that wealth alone was not a measure of God's blessing upon their lives. Nevertheless, the point remains, that if God promised to give His servants a full supply, so that they never experienced any lack, then God will do no less for His children.

God's view of prosperity

What does it mean to be rich?

2 Corinthians 8:9 "For you know the grace of our Lord Jesus Christ, that though He was rich, yet for your sakes He became poor, that you through His poverty might become rich."

So, what does our Lord mean, when He says to us, that we can become rich in this life? The world's view of being is rich, is having great possessions, i.e. large homes, luxury cars, a large bank balance, etc. But that is not heaven's view at all, for God's view of our being rich, is that we will always have an abundant supply, to meet not only all of our needs, but also be able to assist, in meeting the needs of others.

2 Corinthians 9:8 "And God is able to make all grace abound toward you, that you, always having all sufficiency in all things, may have an abundance for every good work."

We have already looked at the above passage of scripture in an earlier section, but it is pertinent in this section as well, because it highlights for us, God's view of our being rich. From this passage, we see that God's view of our being rich, is that we not only have enough to meet our own needs, but that we also have more than enough, so that we can bless others that are themselves in need. And we are to remain in that state at all times. In other words, we are not meant to experience any lack, in our lives.

God's view of prosperity

Philippians 4:19 "And my God shall supply all your need according to His riches in glory by Christ Jesus."

The above passage of scripture, again confirms to us that God's view of our being rich, is that all of our needs are met, and He has promised to do exactly that. And so, the question then arises, as to just what our needs are? As we will see from scripture, God deems our needs to be food, clothing, and a home to live in. In other words, God has promised to provide all the basic requirements that we need, to live in this life, i.e. we should never experience hunger or thirst, we should never be poorly clothed, and we should never be homeless. And so, if these needs are being met, then we should learn to be content with that, for He has promised to never leave us nor forsake us (Hebrews 13:5).

Matthew 6:24-33 "No one can serve two masters; for either he will hate the one and love the other, or else he will be loyal to the one and despise the other. You cannot serve God and mammon. (25) "Therefore, I say to you, do not worry about your life, what you will eat or what you will drink; nor about your body, what you will put on. Is not life more than food and the body more than clothing? (26) Look at the birds of the air, for they neither sow nor reap nor gather into barns; yet your heavenly Father feeds them. Are you not of more value than they? (27) Which of you by worrying can add one cubit to his stature? (28) "So why do you worry about clothing? Consider the lilies of the field, how they grow: they neither toil nor spin; (29) and yet I say to you that even Solomon in all his glory was not

God's view of prosperity

arrayed like one of these. (30) Now if God so clothes the grass of the field, which today is, and tomorrow is thrown into the oven, will He not much more clothe you, O you of little faith? (31) "Therefore, do not worry, saying, 'What shall we eat?' or 'What shall we drink?' or 'What shall we wear?' (32) For after all these things the Gentiles seek. For your heavenly Father knows that you need all these things. (33) But seek first the kingdom of God and His righteousness, and all these things shall be added to you."

We have seen in this section so far, that God has promised to supply all of our needs, to live in this life. And in the above passage of scripture, our Lord Jesus reveals to us, that our heavenly Father knows the things we have need of, in order for us to live in this life. In this passage, our Lord lists two of those needs, i.e. food and clothing. When our Lord mentions these needs, He points us to the way God supplies the needs of His creation, in that they do not sow, reap, gather into barns, toil or spin, and yet God supplies all of their needs. And so, our Lord admonishes us not to worry about our needs, because if God is able to meet the needs of His creation, how much more can He meet our needs, through our sowing, reaping, gathering into barns, toiling and spinning.

Mark 10:28-30 "Then Peter began to say to Him, "See, we have left all and followed You." (29) So Jesus answered and said, "Assuredly, I say to you, there is no one who has left house or brothers or sisters or father or mother or wife or children or lands, for My sake and the gospel's, (30) who shall not receive a hundredfold now in this time--houses

God's view of prosperity

and brothers and sisters and mothers and children and lands, with persecutions--and in the age to come, eternal life."

Our basic needs in this life, also include having a place to live, and in the above passage of scripture, the Lord Jesus confirms to us, that included in our needs being met, is that God provides a home for His children to live in. For in this passage, our Lord speaks of lands and houses. In context, our Lord is speaking about those whom He calls to the ministry, leaving their lands and houses to follow Him. Our Lord tells us that those who are obedient to leave their homes to serve Him, will in this life, receive a hundredfold. The hundredfold that our Lord is speaking about in this passage, pertains to brothers, sisters, mothers and children. For obviously, our Lord adds to those in the ministry, the saints that He has predestined to be included in the sphere of their ministries (2 Corinthians 10:13). The hundredfold lands and houses that our Lord is speaking about, pertains to the Lord's ministers being received into the homes, of all the saints that our Lord has included in their spheres of ministry. It is only the Lord's ministers that are called to leave their homes to serve Him, however not all ministers are called to do that, for even the Lord's apostles had their own homes (John 20:10). But the point that I wanted to raise from this passage, is that our Lord expects His saints to have their own homes, so that His ministers will have a place to stay, when they go out to preach the gospel. And our Lord would not expect His saints to have their own homes, if having their own homes, was not included in their needs, that God has promised to supply.

God's view of prosperity

Matthew 6:8 "Therefore do not be like them. For your Father knows the things you have need of before you ask Him."

We have seen so far in this section, that God's view of our being rich, is that all of our needs are met, and that we actually have an abundance, so that we can bless others with our excess. Although the scriptures, specifically refer to food, clothing and a home to live in, as being the needs that God will supply, as we can see from the above passage of scripture, God understands that our needs extend to things like, transport, education costs, etc, and so these aspects of our needs, are included in that which God supplies.

1 Timothy 6:6-8 "Now godliness with contentment is great gain. (7) For we brought nothing into this world, and it is certain we can carry nothing out. (8) And having food and clothing, with these we shall be content."

In the above passage of scripture, the Holy Spirit through the apostle Paul, also confirms to us what our Lord Jesus has taught us, i.e. that God will supply our basic needs, and if those needs are being met, then as believers, we should be content. However, if our basic needs are not being met, then something is wrong, and we cannot be content. And so, if believers find that their basic needs are not being met, then they need to take stock of their lives, because there is something that they are doing, or not doing, that is preventing God from meeting their needs, for God cannot lie, and He has said that He would supply all of our needs.

God's view of prosperity

Contentment versus covetousness

Hebrews 13:5 "Let your conduct be without covetousness; be content with such things as you have. For He Himself has said, "I will never leave you not forsake you."

We have seen in the previous section, that God's view of our being rich, is that we will always have a full supply, and that we do not experience any lack. And so, if our basic needs are being met, then as believers, we should learn to be content with that. Where many believers get themselves into trouble, is when they see others around them having more than they do, and so they begin to covet. The above passage of scripture counsels us as believers, to be content with that which we have, and not to covet that which we do not have. Because when we do that, we are saying to God, that we are not satisfied with that which He has given us, and that we want more. When believers step outside of contentment, and they step into covetousness, then they step outside of God's provision, and they open themselves up to all sorts of pain and heartache.

Luke 12:15 "And He said to them, "Take heed and beware of covetousness, for one's life does not consist in the abundance of the things he possesses."

When our Lord Jesus went to the cross for us, there were a number of blessings that He purchased for us. One of them was divine health, for the scripture says that by His stripes we were healed (1 Peter 2:24). For those saints

God's view of prosperity

who choose to believe this scripture, and appropriate it for themselves, they will experience walking in divine health. Once one is walking in divine health, that's as far as you can go. You cannot get any healthier, than to walk free from sickness and disease. One of the other blessings, that our Lord purchased for us when He went to the cross, is that He became poor, so that we could become rich (2 Corinthians 8:9). And so, in the same manner, for those saints who choose to believe this scripture, and appropriate it for themselves, they will experience walking free from lack. But I want you to notice from the above passage of scripture, that our Lord warns us in this area, for unlike the area of divine health, once all your needs are met, there is always the temptation to obtain more, and believers need to guard themselves against that.

1 Timothy 6:3-11 "If anyone teaches otherwise and does not consent to wholesome words, even the words of our Lord Jesus Christ, and to the doctrine which accords with godliness, (4) he is proud, knowing nothing, but is obsessed with disputes and arguments over words, from which come envy, strife, reviling, evil suspicions, (5) useless wranglings of men of corrupt minds and destitute of the truth, who suppose that godliness is a means of gain. From such withdraw yourself. (6) Now godliness with contentment is great gain. (7) For we brought nothing into this world, and it is certain we can carry nothing out. (8) And having food and clothing, with these we shall be content. (9) But those who desire to be rich fall into temptation and a snare, and into many foolish and harmful lusts which drown men in destruction and perdition. (10) For the love of money is a root of all kinds of evil, for

God's view of prosperity

which some have strayed from the faith in their greediness and pierced themselves through with many sorrows. (11) But you, O man of God, flee these things and pursue righteousness, godliness, faith, love, patience, gentleness."

In the above passage of scripture, the Holy Spirit through the apostle Paul, also confirms to us, our Lord's warning in this area. For He tells us plainly that we are to be content with having our needs met, and that we should avoid the temptation of wanting to be rich. This passage clearly contrasts God's view of riches, with those of the world, for it is the world that loves money, and are never satisfied with that which they have. Believers that desire riches, as the world does, will be tempted to stray from the faith, through greed, for they become deceived into thinking that godliness is a means of gain. So, what does the apostle Paul mean, when he says that some suppose that godliness is a means of gain? He is talking about those who teach, that there are certain biblical principles, which if applied, will make the believer rich, in worldly terms. And so, you see those ministries catering to those in the church, who have a love for money. Invariably, it is only those who teach that doctrine, that become rich however, because they persuade many in the church to donate to their ministries or buy their materials, but the individual saints themselves, never become wealthy.

Matthew 13:22 "Now he who received seed among the thorns is he who hears the word, and the cares of this world and the deceitfulness of riches choke the word, and he becomes unfruitful."

God's view of prosperity

In the above passage of scripture, our Lord Jesus teaches us that riches in this life are deceitful, for they choke the word in the life of the believer, and those believers become unfruitful in the kingdom of God. The reason that riches in this life are deceitful, is because although the believer may be rich, wealthy, and have need of nothing in the natural, because they have become unfruitful in the kingdom of God, they are in fact wretched, miserable, poor, blind, and naked in the spirit (Revelation 3:17). There can be no doubt, that for believers to seek after riches in this life, is very foolish indeed.

James 4:1-3 "Where do wars and fights come from among you? Do they not come from your desires for pleasure that war in your members? (2) You lust and do not have. You murder and covet and cannot obtain. You fight and war. Yet you do not have because you do not ask. (3) You ask and do not receive, because you ask amiss, that you may spend it on your pleasures."

In the above passage of scripture, the Holy Spirit through the apostle James, teaches us the difference between asking God to meet our needs, and asking Him for riches. Clearly from this passage, the inference is that when we ask for our needs to be met, that God will supply those needs. But it is also clearly stated, that God will not answer prayer requests that ask for riches. And so, we once again see, the difference between God's view of our being rich in this life, and the carnal view of being rich, and those views are completely opposite to each other.

God's view of prosperity

Chapter 3
New testament examples

Jesus' early years

Hebrews 12:1-2 "Therefore we also, since we are surrounded by so great a cloud of witnesses, let us lay aside every weight, and the sin which so easily ensnares us, and let us run with endurance the race that is set before us, (2) looking unto Jesus, the author and finisher of our faith, who for the joy that was set before Him endured the cross, despising the shame, and has sat down at the right hand of the throne of God."

In everything we do, we should always look at our Lord Jesus, as our ultimate example that we should follow. The Holy Spirit in the above passage of scripture, teaches us that we should look at Jesus, the author and finisher of our faith. In other words, Jesus is our example, and we should live our lives as He did, when He was on the earth, and that would include the area of prospering in this life. We have already established that it is the will of God our Father, that we walk in prosperity, and if Jesus walked in God's perfect will, then He must have experienced God's prosperity being made manifest in, and through, His life. So, we want to look at accounts in scripture, that will reveal to us, just how Jesus walked in this area.

Matthew 2:1-11 "Now after Jesus was born in Bethlehem of Judea in the days of Herod the king,

New testament examples

behold, wise men from the East came to Jerusalem, (2) saying, "Where is He who has been born King of the Jews? For we have seen His star in the East and have come to worship Him." ... (11) And when they had come into the house, they saw the young Child with Mary His mother, and fell down and worshiped Him. And when they had opened their treasures, they presented gifts to Him: gold, frankincense, and myrrh."

Many who teach the "prosperity gospel" to the extreme, refer to the above passage of scripture, to prove that Jesus was born into a wealthy home. They do so, by claiming that the gifts of gold, frankincense, and myrrh that were brought by the wise men from the east, was God's supernatural provision for His Son, which amounted to a substantial sum of money. I have heard one very well-known preacher on TV, estimating the value of gifts given, at being equal to the staggering amount of forty million dollars, because the wise men apparently arrived with a camel train load, of gifts for the Lord. Clearly, the imagination of the carnal mind knows no limits, when it comes to the desire for riches. So, what does bible actually teach us regarding this incident?

Luke 2:21-24 "And when eight days were completed for the circumcision of the Child, His name was called Jesus, the name given by the angel before He was conceived in the womb. (22) Now when the days of her purification according to the law of Moses were completed, they brought Him to Jerusalem to present Him to the Lord (23) (as it is written in the law of the Lord, "Every male who opens the womb shall be called holy to the Lord"),

New testament examples

(24) and to offer a sacrifice according to what is said in the law of the Lord, "A pair of turtledoves or two young pigeons."

The wise men from the east, had come to see our Lord Jesus, while He was still in the town of Bethlehem. Joseph and Mary remained in Bethlehem after Jesus was born, while they waited for the days of Mary's purification according to the law of Moses, to be completed, which was a period of forty days. After those days were fulfilled, Joseph and Mary then took our Lord Jesus to the temple in Jerusalem, to present Him to God the Father. At the same time, Mary was required to offer a cleansing sacrifice for herself in the temple, which was the sacrifice referred to in the above passage of scripture. It is this sacrifice, that gives us insight into the financial status of Joseph and Mary at the time, for this was after they had received the gifts of gold, frankincense, and myrrh, from the wise men. The Holy Spirit, in this passage of scripture, records that they offered a pair of turtledoves or two young pigeons.

Leviticus 12:1-7 "Then the Lord spoke to Moses, saying, (2) "Speak to the children of Israel, saying: 'If a woman has conceived, and borne a male child, then she shall be unclean seven days; as in the days of her customary impurity she shall be unclean. (3) And on the eighth day the flesh of his foreskin shall be circumcised. (4) She shall then continue in the blood of her purification thirty-three days. She shall not touch any hallowed thing, nor come into the sanctuary until the days of her purification are fulfilled. ... (6) 'When the days of her purification are fulfilled, whether for a son or a daughter, she shall

New testament examples

bring to the priest a lamb of the first year as a burnt offering, and a young pigeon or a turtledove as a sin offering, to the door of the tabernacle of meeting. (7) Then he shall offer it before the Lord and make atonement for her. And she shall be clean from the flow of her blood. This is the law for her who has borne a male or a female."

The above passage of scripture teaches us, that the offering that God required from Mary, was that she was to bring to the priest, a lamb of the first year as a burnt offering, and a young pigeon or a turtledove as a sin offering. And yet we have seen in the account in Luke's gospel, that Mary and Joseph offered a pair of turtledoves or two young pigeons. So why did they not offer the sacrifice that God required? The answer to that question lies in the following passage of scripture.

Leviticus 12:8 "'And if she is not able to bring a lamb, then she may bring two turtledoves or two young pigeons--one as a burnt offering and the other as a sin offering. So, the priest shall make atonement for her, and she will be clean.'"

And so, we can see that in the law of Moses, for those who could not afford to offer a lamb (Leviticus 14:21-22), God had made provision for them, to offer two turtledoves or two young pigeons instead, and that offering would be acceptable to the Lord. Joseph and Mary obviously could not afford to offer a lamb to the Lord, and so they presented the offering that they could afford, which clearly reveals to us, that Joseph and Mary were not wealthy by any stretch of the imagination, and that the gifts that the wise men brought, would have only

New testament examples

been token in nature. And so, we can see from scripture, that our Lord Jesus was not born into a wealthy home, as some would have us to believe.

> *Mark 6:3 "Is this not the carpenter, the Son of Mary, and brother of James, Joses, Judas, and Simon? And are not His sisters here with us?" So, they were offended at Him."*

The scriptures are silent on most of Jesus life on the earth, before the baptism of John. We have the account of our Lord's birth, and the incident that occurred when He was twelve years old, but other than that, we are not told very much else. But there is some information, that the Holy Spirit imparts to us in the above passage of scripture, that gives us a bit of insight into our Lord's life, before He began His public ministry. The context of this passage, is that Jesus had gone back to His hometown of Nazareth, where He had grown up, and He had preached in the local synagogue for the first time. From this passage, we see that Jesus grew up in a relatively large home, for He had seven siblings. But we also see that Jesus had worked with his father Joseph, in the family's carpentry business. We know that Jesus would have excelled in that trade, for the scripture tells us that Jesus did all things well (Mark 7:37), and so there is no reason to believe that the family business, would not have been blessed by the Lord, and prosperous. But even though the family business must have prospered, Nazareth was not a very large town, and so the business would have only generated sufficient revenue for the Lord's family to live a comfortable lifestyle, nothing more. And this agrees with what God had promised to provide for the children of Israel.

New testament examples

Jesus' home

Matthew 9:28 "And when He had come into <u>the house</u>, the blind men came to Him. And Jesus said to them, "Do you believe that I am able to do this?" They said to Him, "Yes, Lord."

Matthew 13:1-36 "On the same day Jesus went out of <u>the house</u> and sat by the sea ... (36) Then Jesus sent the multitude away and went into <u>the house</u>. And His disciples came to Him, saying, "Explain to us the parable of the tares of the field."

Matthew 17:24-26 "When they had come to Capernaum, those who received the tax came to Peter and said, "Does your Teacher not pay the tax?" (25) He said, "Yes." And when he had come into <u>the house</u>, Jesus anticipated him, saying, "What do you think, Simon? From whom do the kings of the earth take customs or taxes, from their sons or from strangers?" (26) Peter said to Him, "From strangers." Jesus said to him, "Then the sons are free."

Mark 2:1 "And again He entered Capernaum after some days, and it was heard that He was in <u>the house</u>."

Mark 9:28-33 "And when He had come into <u>the house</u>, His disciples asked Him privately, "Why could we not cast it out?" (29) So, He said to them, "This kind can come out by nothing but prayer and fasting." (30) Then they departed from there and passed through Galilee, and He did not want anyone

New testament examples

to know it. ... (33) Then He came to Capernaum. And when He was in <u>the house</u> He asked them, "What was it you disputed among yourselves on the road?"

     Our Lord Jesus lived in the town of Nazareth for most of His life. But when He entered into the ministry, He and His family relocated to the town of Capernaum (Matthew 4:13), which was a town roughly three times the size of Nazareth. Our Lord Jesus began His public ministry at the age of thirty-eight (refer to my book, "The Body of Man" for more details about the Lord's age), and by that time He was already living on His own. All of the above quoted scriptures, refer to the house that our Lord lived in, while He was in Capernaum. This was the same house, that had the tiling removed by the four men who let their paralyzed friend down through the roof, to be healed by the Lord (Mark 2:9-11). It was also this house, which Mary and her sons stood outside, wanting to speak to Jesus (Mark 3:31). But I want you to notice that the scripture always refers to the home that the Lord lived in, as the "the house", and not "His house". The reason for that, is because the house that our Lord lived in was not His own, but rather one that He rented. This is why our Lord made the comment about Himself that, "Foxes have holes and birds of the air have nests, but the Son of Man has nowhere to lay His head" (Matthew 8:20). This agrees with what the apostle Paul said about himself, for he also described himself as one who was homeless (1 Corinthians 4:11). And yet we know that Paul did from time to time, rent his own home to live in (Acts 28:30). So, does this mean that our Lord Jesus does not want His saints, to own their homes? Not at all, for as we have already said, our Lord Jesus only expects His ministers of the gospel, to be prepared to leave all that they have to follow Him, and

New testament examples

as such, Jesus has shown them the way, through His example. But the point that I want to raise in this section, is that included in the needs of our Lord Jesus, that God the Father took care of, was a house for His Son to live in, and God continues to do the same thing for each of His children today.

Jesus' generosity

John 2:1-10 "On the third day there was a wedding in Cana of Galilee, and the mother of Jesus was there. (2) Now both Jesus and His disciples were invited to the wedding. (3) And when they ran out of wine, the mother of Jesus said to Him, "They have no wine." (4) Jesus said to her, "Woman, what does your concern have to do with Me? My hour has not yet come." (5) His mother said to the servants, "Whatever He says to you, do it." (6) Now there were set there six water pots of stone, according to the manner of purification of the Jews, containing twenty or thirty gallons apiece. (7) Jesus said to them, "Fill the water pots with water." And they filled them up to the brim. (8) And He said to them, "Draw some out now, and take it to the master of the feast." And they took it. (9) When the master of the feast had tasted the water that was made wine and did not know where it came from (but the servants who had drawn the water knew), the master of the feast called the bridegroom. (10) And he said to him, "Every man at the beginning sets out the good wine, and when the guests have well drunk, then the inferior. You have kept the good wine until now!"

New testament examples

The above passage of scripture, is a very clear account of the generosity of our Lord Jesus. The context of this passage, is that Jesus was attending His younger sister's wedding, for the reason that Jesus was allowed to invite His disciples to the wedding, was because He was the bride's older brother. And that is also the reason that Mary became involved, with the issue that had arisen with the wine running out, for it was her daughter and new son-in-law, that were about to be embarrassed in front of their guests. We are all familiar with the above account, of how our Lord turned the water into wine, and our natural thinking is that Jesus saved them from embarrassment, by performing this miracle. But there is more to it than that, for in effect, through this miracle, Jesus blessed the newlywed couple with a wedding gift. The reason that I made the comment, that this account shows the generosity of our Lord, is because when we calculate the quantity and quality of the wine that Jesus blessed them with, we see that this wedding gift equated to approximately seventy-five thousand rand in today's value. And so, even though it was Jesus younger sister, the value of the gift was still extremely generous.

Luke 5:3-9 "Then He got into one of the boats, which was Simon's, and asked him to put out a little from the land. And He sat down and taught the multitudes from the boat. (4) When He had stopped speaking, He said to Simon, "Launch out into the deep and let down your nets for a catch." (5) But Simon answered and said to Him, "Master, we have toiled all night and caught nothing; nevertheless, at Your word I will let down the net." (6) And when they had done this, they caught a great number of fish, and their net was breaking. (7) So, they

New testament examples

signalled to their partners in the other boat to come and help them. And they came and filled both the boats, so that they began to sink. (8) When Simon Peter saw it, he fell down at Jesus' knees, saying, "Depart from me, for I am a sinful man, O Lord!" (9) For he and all who were with him were astonished at the catch of fish which they had taken."

The above passage of scripture, is another very clear account of the generosity of our Lord Jesus. The context of this passage, is that our Lord had borrowed Peter's boat to use it as a platform, from which He could preach the gospel to the multitudes. It could not have been more than a couple of hours, that He made use of Peter's boat, but when our Lord had finished, He paid Peter for the use of his boat. Again, we all know the account of how our Lord worked a miracle, through the multitude of fish that Peter and his colleagues caught, and in our natural thinking, we focus on the miracle. But the reason that I say that this act also demonstrated our Lord's generosity, is because of the value of the payment that He made. For when we calculate the quantity of fish that was caught on that day, it equates to approximately one hundred and sixty thousand rand in today's value. That is an extremely generous payment, for a couple of hours use of Peter's boat.

Mark 6:37-42 "But He answered and said to them, "You give them something to eat." And they said to Him, "Shall we go and buy two hundred denarii worth of bread and give them something to eat?" (38) But He said to them, "How many loaves do you have? Go and see." And when they found out they said, "Five, and two fish." (39) Then He

New testament examples

commanded them to make them all sit down in groups on the green grass. (40) So, they sat down in ranks, in hundreds and in fifties. (41) And when He had taken the five loaves and the two fish, He looked up to heaven, blessed and broke the loaves, and gave them to His disciples to set before them; and the two fish He divided among them all. (42) So, they all ate and were filled."

Again, in the above passage of scripture, we see another account of the generosity of our Lord Jesus. This is the account in scripture, when our Lord fed the five thousand. In the natural, it would have taken roughly half a million rand in today's value, to be able to buy enough food, to feed that many people, so that all were filled. And the scripture says that all were filled. So clearly, our Lord was more than generous, with the way that He fed the multitudes.

John 21:5-11 "Then Jesus said to them, "Children, have you any food?" They answered Him, "No." (6) And He said to them, "Cast the net on the right side of the boat, and you will find some." So, they cast, and now they were not able to draw it in because of the multitude of fish. (7) Therefore, that disciple whom Jesus loved said to Peter, "It is the Lord!" Now when Simon Peter heard that it was the Lord, he put on his outer garment (for he had removed it) and plunged into the sea. (8) But the other disciples came in the little boat (for they were not far from land, but about two hundred cubits), dragging the net with fish. (9) Then, as soon as they had come to land, they saw a fire of coals there, and fish laid on it, and bread. (10) Jesus said to them,

New testament examples

"Bring some of the fish which you have just caught." (11) Simon Peter went up and dragged the net to land, full of large fish, one hundred and fifty-three; and although there were so many, the net was not broken."

The above passage of scripture, is another very clear account of the generosity of our Lord Jesus. For when we calculate the quantity of fish that was caught on that day, it equates to approximately forty thousand rand in today's value. It is important for us to see these examples of our Lord's generosity, because it reveals to us just how generous God our Father is, for our Lord and the Father are one. And so, we see that God is not stingy, and when He blesses an individual, then He does so generously.

Jesus' ministry finances

Mark 6:37-42 "But He answered and said to them, "You give them something to eat." And they said to Him, "Shall we go and buy two hundred denarii worth of bread and give them something to eat?" (38) But He said to them, "How many loaves do you have? Go and see." And when they found out they said, "Five, and two fish." (39) Then He commanded them to make them all sit down in groups on the green grass. (40) So, they sat down in ranks, in hundreds and in fifties. (41) And when He had taken the five loaves and the two fish, He looked up to heaven, blessed and broke the loaves, and gave them to His disciples to set before them; and the two fish He divided among them all. (42) So, they all ate and were filled."

New testament examples

We have already looked at the above miracle in the previous section, to show our Lord's generosity, but there is something else that is revealed to us in this passage of scripture, regarding the financial aspect of our Lord's ministry. For I want you to notice, that the disciples stated that two hundred denarii was not enough, to purchase food for that multitude. The reason the disciples made that comment, was because that's the amount of money that they had on hand at the time. In today's value, that amount equated to approximately one hundred thousand rand, and as we have already seen, that was not enough money to buy food for that size crowd. But the point that I wanted to get across from this passage, is that at the time, there was two hundred denarii in the money box that Judas carried. So where did that amount of money come from? After our Lord Jesus left the family's carpentry business to preach the gospel, He no longer earned an income as a carpenter, and so He had to have another source of income. Our Lord Jesus, as the Head of the church, has commanded that those who preach the gospel, are to live from the gospel (1 Corinthians 9:14). And as the Head of the church, our Lord Jesus practiced what He preached, and so as one who preached the gospel, our Lord Jesus lived from the gospel.

Luke 8:1-3 "Now it came to pass, afterward, that He went through every city and village, preaching and bringing the glad tidings of the kingdom of God. And the twelve were with Him, (2) and certain women who had been healed of evil spirits and infirmities--Mary called Magdalene, out of whom had come seven demons, (3) and Joanna the wife of Chuza, Herod's steward, and Susanna,

New testament examples

and many others who provided for Him from their substance."

From the above passage of scripture, the Holy Spirit reveals to us that there were many that God the Father raised up, to financially support our Lord's ministry, when He was on the earth, and some of those individuals were very wealthy. For example, Lazarus, Mary and Martha, were three siblings that had inherited a substantial amount of wealth from their parents. You will recall the incident when Mary poured the alabaster flask of spikenard on our Lord Jesus, before He went to the cross (Mark 14:3-5). That flask could have been sold for three hundred denarii, which equates to approximately one hundred and fifty thousand rand in today's value. For Mary to own such expensive oil, is a clear indication as to just how wealthy they were. We read the account, of our Lord inviting the rich young man to sell all he had, to give to the poor and follow Him (Matthew 19:21), and we think erroneously, that our Lord instructed all rich people, to do the same. But that is not the case at all, because Jesus only encouraged those whom He called to follow Him in ministry, to leave all and follow Him. Zacchaeus would be another case in point, because he only gave half of his wealth away and kept the rest (which was still a substantial amount of wealth), and our Lord said of Zacchaeus, that salvation had come to his home, i.e. he became one of the Lord's disciples (Luke 19:9). And so, it was because of individuals like that giving into our Lord's ministry, that there was an amount of one hundred thousand rand in the money box, at the time that Jesus fed the five thousand. Now, that would not have been the only occasion when our Lord's ministry carried that amount of money with them, but rather, that would have

New testament examples

been the norm for His ministries finances at any given point in time. So why would our Lord have needed that much money, at any one time? The answer to that question, is that Jesus had a very large ministry team that walked with Him. It was not just the twelve apostles that walked with the Lord, for you will recall that He sent out seventy disciples at one time to minister (Luke 10:1). And when Jesus called His disciples to follow Him, He would always instruct them to leave all behind (Mark 10:21), and many of our Lord's disciples had families to support. And so, the finances that came into Jesus ministry, were used by Him, to supply the needs of His disciples, and their families. And so, during our Lord's two years of ministry on the earth, there were vast amounts of money, that were given into His ministry.

> *John 13:29 "For some thought, because Judas had the money box, that Jesus had said to him, "Buy those things we need for the feast," or that he should give something to the poor."*

Although Judas controlled the money box, he used that money, at the instruction of Jesus. The above passage of scripture, reveals to us that Jesus would instruct Judas, what to purchase on behalf of Jesus and His ministry team. But this passage also reveals to us, that the finances that came into our Lord's ministry, were not solely used to supply the needs of His disciples, but also to minister to the poor. It was not uncommon, for our Lord to instruct Judas to give to the poor, at all hours of the day. It was late at night in the above account, when the other disciples naturally assumed, that Jesus had instructed Judas to go and give to the poor. In fact, it seems that the majority of the money given into our Lord's ministry, was

New testament examples

given to the poor. For when the disciples complained about the extravagant waste of money, when Mary poured the expensive fragrant oil on our Lord, their comment was not that the money could have been used to supply their needs, but rather given to the poor (John 12:5), thus indicating that the norm in our Lord's ministry, was to give to the poor. And so, in the above accounts, we have seen just how generous our Lord Jesus was toward others, and we have seen how He supplied the needs of all His disciples. And we have also seen, just how frequently, Jesus gave to the poor.

Jesus' personal finances

Luke 12:22-28 "Then He said to His disciples, "Therefore I say to you, do not worry about your life, what you will eat; nor about the body, what you will put on. (23) Life is more than food, and the body is more than clothing. (24) Consider the ravens, for they neither sow nor reap, which have neither storehouse nor barn; and God feeds them. Of how much more value are you than the birds? (25) And which of you by worrying can add one cubit to his stature? (26) If you then are not able to do the least, why are you anxious for the rest? (27) Consider the lilies, how they grow: they neither toil nor spin; and yet I say to you, even Solomon in all his glory was not arrayed like one of these. (28) If then God so clothes the grass, which today is in the field and tomorrow is thrown into the oven, how much more will He clothe you, O you of little faith?"

So, what about Jesus personal finances? The answer to that question is simple. The only thing that

New testament examples

Jesus owned, were the clothes that He wore, and absolutely nothing else. Our Lord Jesus is not a hypocrite. In the above passage of scripture, He taught us that just as God supplied the needs of all His creation, so He would supply all of our needs. And so, our Lord Jesus lived exactly like that. He lived, as the birds of the air live, having full confidence in God supplying His every need, and never once worrying about His needs being met. During His time of ministry on the earth, Jesus did the work of the ministry, for He understood the principle that if anyone will not work, neither shall he eat (2 Thessalonians 3:10). And so, as He did the work that God the Father had given Him to accomplish, He knew that God would take care of all His needs, and never once gave that a second thought.

John 7:53 "And everyone went to his own house."
John 8:1-2 "But Jesus went to the Mount of Olives. (2) Now early in the morning He came again into the temple, and all the people came to Him; and He sat down and taught them."

Jesus never owned a home, but we have seen earlier, that Jesus rented a house in Capernaum. Nevertheless, many times during our Lord Jesus ministry, He would sleep under the stars, and His disciples would follow suit. The above scriptures, are clearly illustrative of this point. For it states, that all the Jews went to their own houses, but Jesus went to the mount of Olives, where He slept under the stars, and returned in the morning, to teach in the temple. When Jesus travelled around ministering, and He was not staying in the open, He would stay in the houses of those, who had invited Him

New testament examples

into their homes. He stayed in Peter's home (Luke 4:38), He stayed in Simon the leper's home (Matthew 26:6), He stayed in Levi's home (Mark 2:15), He stayed in Martha and Mary's home (John 12:1-2), and I am sure that there are many other homes that our Lord stayed in, as He travelled around Judea and Galilee, proclaiming the gospel. But the point that I wanted to highlight in this section, is that when He dwelt on the earth, our Lord Jesus did not have a home of His own, that He owned.

> *Matthew 17:24-27 "When they had come to Capernaum, those who received the tax came to Peter and said, "Does your Teacher not pay the tax?" (25) He said, "Yes." And when he had come into the house, Jesus anticipated him, saying, "What do you think, Simon? From whom do the kings of the earth take customs or taxes, from their sons or from strangers?" (26) Peter said to Him, "From strangers." Jesus said to him, "Then the sons are free. (27) Nevertheless, lest we offend them, go to the sea, cast in a hook, and take the fish that comes up first. And when you have opened its mouth, you will find a piece of money; take that and give it to them for Me and you."*

We have already seen that there were vast amounts of money that passed through Jesus ministry. Nevertheless, He never once used any of that money, for His own personal use. The above passage of scripture, illustrates this point. For those who collected the government taxes, approached Peter regarding our Lord's tax obligations. Our Lord knew what had transpired, before Peter spoke to Him about the issue. And so, He had already exercised His faith in God, to obtain the necessary

New testament examples

funds in order to meet His (and Peter's) tax obligations, which resulted in God dispatching a fish, to retrieve that money lying on the ocean floor. But the point that I wanted to highlight from this account, is that Jesus did not use the ministry funds, to pay His personal tax bill.

Luke 19:29-35 "And it came to pass, when He drew near to Bethphage and Bethany, at the mountain called Olivet, that He sent two of His disciples, (30) saying, "Go into the village opposite you, where as you enter you will find a colt tied, on which no one has ever sat. Loose it and bring it here. (31) And if anyone asks you, 'Why are you loosing it?' thus you shall say to him, 'Because the Lord has need of it.' " (32) So those who were sent went their way and found it just as He had said to them. (33) But as they were loosing the colt, the owners of it said to them, "Why are you loosing the colt?" (34) And they said, "The Lord has need of him." (35) Then they brought him to Jesus. And they threw their own clothes on the colt, and they set Jesus on him."

Zechariah 9:9 "Rejoice greatly, O daughter of Zion! Shout, O daughter of Jerusalem! Behold, your King is coming to you; He is just and having salvation, Lowly and riding on a donkey, A colt, the foal of a donkey."

Even when our Lord Jesus fulfilled the scriptures, by riding into the city of Jerusalem on a donkey, He did that on a borrowed donkey, for other than the clothes that He wore, our Lord owned absolutely nothing in this life. Those who would distort the gospel, to justify their own

New testament examples

love of money, have said that when Jesus rode into Jerusalem on a donkey, that it was the best mode of transportation in our Lord's day, and as such, it was the equivalent of driving in a luxury vehicle today. That is obviously nonsense, for the wealthy people in our Lord's day, rode in chariots (Acts 8:12), on horseback, or they were carried by slaves in litters. And so, those who would distort the gospel, forget that the Holy Spirit has said that our Lord came to the city of Jerusalem, <u>lowly</u> and riding on a donkey, i.e. He showed His humility in this act.

Mark 15:24 "And when they crucified Him, they divided His garments, casting lots for them to determine what every man should take."

Psalms 22:17-18 "I can count all My bones. They look and stare at Me. (18) They divide My garments among them, And for My clothing they cast lots."

I have already stated that all that our Lord Jesus owned, when He walked this earth, were the clothes that He wore. The above passages of scripture confirm this, for when He hung on the cross, it was for His clothes, that the Roman soldiers cast lots, to see who would take them for himself. And so, we see clearly, that in this life, Jesus was what the world would call, a poor, homeless, man. But even though Jesus never owned anything, He still lived this life, never lacking anything, for God the Father, took care of His every need.

The Lord's ministers

New testament examples

Luke 9:1-4 "Then He called His twelve disciples together and gave them power and authority over all demons, and to cure diseases. (2) He sent them to preach the kingdom of God and to heal the sick. (3) And He said to them, "Take nothing for the journey, neither staffs nor bag nor bread nor money; and do not have two tunics apiece. (4) "Whatever house you enter, stay there, and from there depart."

The lifestyle that Jesus practiced, He taught to His disciples. And so, when He sent out the twelve apostles to minister on their own for the first time, He was very clear in His instructions, as to how they were to go out to minister. He did not allow them to take anything with them, only the clothes that they wore. So why did He do that? Well, as we have already seen, that is the way that our Lord Jesus ministered, and He wanted His disciples to learn to trust in God's provision, just as He did.

Luke 10:1-8 "After these things the Lord appointed seventy others also and sent them two by two before His face into every city and place where He Himself was about to go. (2) Then He said to them, "The harvest truly is great, but the laborers are few; therefore, pray the Lord of the harvest to send out laborers into His harvest. (3) Go your way; behold, I send you out as lambs among wolves. (4) Carry neither money bag, knapsack, nor sandals; and greet no one along the road. (5) But whatever house you enter, first say, 'Peace to this house.' (6) And if a son of peace is there, your peace will rest on it; if not, it will return to you. (7) And remain in the same house, eating and drinking such

New testament examples

things as they give, for the labourer is worthy of his wages. Do not go from house to house. (8) Whatever city you enter, and they receive you, eat such things as are set before you."

Later in our Lord's ministry, He also sent out the seventy, to minister on their own. Notice the instructions that He gave them. Those instructions were exactly the same, that He had given to the twelve, when they went out to minister. For they also, were not allowed to take anything with them, only the clothes that they wore. They were to stay in the homes of those who invited them to stay, and they were to eat the food that their hosts put before them, being thankful for that which was provided. And so, when they went out to minister the gospel, it was the very same lifestyle that Jesus practiced, which He taught His disciples to follow.

Luke 22:35 "And He said to them, "When I sent you without money bag, knapsack, and sandals, did you lack anything?" So, they said, "Nothing."

As we saw earlier in this teaching, when the disciples walked with the Lord, that He took care of all of their needs, and they never lacked for anything. But when our Lord sent the disciples out on their own, He wanted them to learn to trust in God's provision for themselves. And as we can see from the above passage of scripture, the disciples had learnt that lesson, for they stated that they lacked nothing when they went out on their own. So, does this mean that Jesus expects all of His saints to live in this manner today? The answer to that question is, no. That which our Lord taught His disciples in this area, is for those who are called to minister the gospel, for that is the

New testament examples

work that He has given them to do, which is why He says, that the labourer is worthy of his wages. One who works, earns wages. Those whom our Lord calls to the ministry of His gospel, have the right to forego secular work, so that they can do the work of the ministry (1 Corinthians 9:6). And so, they are to live by the gospel (1 Corinthians 9:14), as God supplies all of their need, even as God supplied our Lord's need, when He ministered on the earth.

1 Timothy 6:6-10 "Now godliness with contentment is great gain. (7) For we brought nothing into this world, and it is certain we can carry nothing out. (8) And having food and clothing, with these we shall be content. (9) But those who desire to be rich fall into temptation and a snare, and into many foolish and harmful lusts which drown men in destruction and perdition. (10) For the love of money is a root of all kinds of evil, for which some have strayed from the faith in their greediness and pierced themselves through with many sorrows."

There is no scriptural evidence, of any of the Lord's ministers becoming very wealthy. On the contrary, there is much evidence that the Lord's ministers preached against excessive wealth. The above passage of scripture, clearly reveals to us the apostle Paul's viewpoint, of riches in this life. Although Paul did tell us that he had learnt how to be abased and how to abound (Philippians 4:12), scriptural evidence is very clear, that the apostle Paul was not, by any stretch of the imagination, a wealthy man. And in fact, he described himself as being poorly clothed and homeless (1 Corinthians 4:11).

New testament examples

> *James 1:9-11 "Let the lowly brother glory in his exaltation, (10) but the rich in his humiliation, because as a flower of the field he will pass away. (11) For no sooner has the sun risen with a burning heat than it withers the grass; its flower falls, and its beautiful appearance perishes. So, the rich man also will fade away in his pursuits."*

As we can see in the above passage of scripture, the apostle James, also has nothing good to say about those who are rich in this life. And in fact, later in his letter, he strongly rebukes the unbelievers that are rich, by telling them that they have lived on the earth in pleasure and luxury; and have fattened their hearts as in a day of slaughter. The Lord's apostle was not a hypocrite, and so James would not have expressed his views so strongly in this area, if he himself, had been one who was wealthy.

> *2 Peter 2:3-15 "By covetousness they will exploit you with deceptive words; for a long time, their judgment has not been idle, and their destruction does not slumber. ... (13) and will receive the wages of unrighteousness, as those who count it pleasure to carouse in the daytime. They are spots and blemishes, carousing in their own deceptions while they feast with you, (14) having eyes full of adultery and that cannot cease from sin, enticing unstable souls. They have a heart trained in covetous practices and are accursed children. (15) They have forsaken the right way and gone astray, following the way of Balaam the son of Beor, who loved the wages of unrighteousness."*

New testament examples

In the above passage of scripture, the apostle Peter teaches the church to avoid those who preach the gospel with deceptive words, using them as a cloak for covetousness. He equates them with Balaam, who loved money, and used his prophetic gift to gain riches in this life. And so, just as in the case of James, the apostle Peter would not have spoken out against covetous practices in the ministry, if he had himself become wealthy, through the ministry gift that he had received from the Lord.

1 John 2:15-16 "Do not love the world or the things in the world. If anyone loves the world, the love of the Father is not in him. (16) For all that is in the world--the lust of the flesh, the lust of the eyes, and the pride of life--is not of the Father but is of the world."

The apostle John, also leaves no doubt as to his viewpoint on riches in this life, for he tells the church not to love the world, or the things in the world. These are the very things that the world loves and pursues, for they love to satisfy their fleshly desires, and they always want more, for they never have enough, and those who do attain wealth, love to display that wealth with pride. Again, the apostle John was not a hypocrite, and he would not have counselled the church to refrain from loving the things in the world, if he himself fell into the category of being one who was considered to be wealthy in this life.

Jude 1:11-13 "Woe to them! For they have gone in the way of Cain, have run greedily in the error of Balaam for profit, and perished in the rebellion of Korah. (12) These are spots in your love feasts, while they feast with you without fear, serving only

New testament examples

themselves. They are clouds without water, carried about by the winds; late autumn trees without fruit, twice dead, pulled up by the roots; (13) raging waves of the sea, foaming up their own shame; wandering stars for whom is reserved the blackness of darkness forever."

In the above passage of scripture, the apostle Jude teaches the church almost word for word, the same admonition that the apostle Peter teaches us, i.e. to avoid those who preach the gospel with the same motive as Balaam, who loved money, and used his prophetic gift to gain riches in this life. And so, the apostle Jude would also not have spoken out against covetous practices in the ministry, if he had himself become wealthy, through the ministry gift that he had received from the Lord.

1 Corinthians 9:4-6 "Do we have no right to eat and drink? (5) Do we have no right to take along a believing wife, as do also the other apostles, the brothers of the Lord, and Cephas? (6) Or is it only Barnabas and I who have no right to refrain from working?"

And so, as we have seen in the previous passages of scripture, the Lord's apostles were not wealthy in this life, and actually warned the church against the desire to become rich in this life. Nevertheless, there is also clear evidence in scripture, that our Lord took care of all His minister's needs, so that they could live comfortable lifestyles. In the above passage of scripture, the apostle Paul alludes to the fact that all of the Lord's apostles, refrained from secular work, and that when they travelled around to the churches, that their wives accompanied

New testament examples

them. And so, clearly the Lord's apostles did not suffer any lack, financially.

> *1 Corinthians 9:12-18 "If others are partakers of this right over you, are we not even more? Nevertheless, we have not used this right, but endure all things lest we hinder the gospel of Christ. (13) Do you not know that those who minister the holy things eat of the things of the temple, and those who serve at the altar partake of the offerings of the altar? (14) Even so the Lord has commanded that those who preach the gospel should live from the gospel. (15) But I have used none of these things, nor have I written these things that it should be done so to me; for it would be better for me to die than that anyone should make my boasting void. (16) For if I preach the gospel, I have nothing to boast of, for necessity is laid upon me; yes, woe is me if I do not preach the gospel! (17) For if I do this willingly, I have a reward; but if against my will, I have been entrusted with a stewardship. (18) What is my reward then? That when I preach the gospel, I may present the gospel of Christ without charge, that I may not abuse my authority in the gospel."*

The apostle Paul and his ministry team however, operated differently to the rest of the Lord's apostles. For even though they had the right to forego secular work, and take up offerings from the churches, so that they could live from the gospel, they chose not to use that right. The apostle Paul explains his reasoning regarding his decision, in the above passage of scripture. For Paul realized that even though he was preaching the gospel, it wasn't costing him anything to do so, for the Lord had given him both

New testament examples

the mandate, and the ability, to preach the gospel. Which is why Paul stated that he could not expect any reward from the Lord on his day of judgement, for simply being obedient to God's call. And so, Paul had decided to preach the gospel, "without charge", and he and his ministry team worked with their own hands to supply their needs, rather than allow the church to do so. Thus, it was costing Paul and his team to preach the gospel, and he could therefore expect the Lord to reward him on his day of judgement. But Paul also limited this aspect of his ministry, to the regions of Achaia only (2 Corinthians 11:10), for he did accept offerings from the churches in Macedonia for example (2 Corinthians 11:9). And so, the point remains, that although the Lord's ministers were not wealthy men according to this world's standards, our Lord Jesus nevertheless, provided for all the needs of His ministers.

1 Timothy 3:1-8 "This is a faithful saying: If a man desires the position of a bishop, he desires a good work. (2) A bishop then must be blameless, the husband of one wife, temperate, sober-minded, of good behaviour, hospitable, able to teach; (3) not given to wine, not violent, not greedy for money, but gentle, not quarrelsome, not covetous; ... (8) Likewise, deacons must be reverent, not double-tongued, not given to much wine, not greedy for money."

In the above passage of scripture, the Holy Spirit sets out the qualifications needed, by those who want to serve in the church, as elders (the word translated bishop can also be translated elder) and deacons. In both instances, the Holy Spirit through the apostle Paul, states

New testament examples

that they are not to be greedy for money. Clearly, if the Lord does not want His elders and deacons to be greedy for money, then His ministers should be exemplary in this area, for they are meant to lead His church by example. The vast majority of the Lord's ministers in the church today, will never be tempted in the area of riches, purely because their churches are themselves not very wealthy. But there are certain churches and ministries in the church today, that do receive vast amounts of finances. It is these ministers, that are tempted in the area of riches. But even among these ministers, there are those who follow after our Lord's example, and live comfortable lifestyles, not accumulating excessive wealth for themselves. However, sadly there are some ministers, who succumb to the temptation of riches and do accumulate vast wealth for themselves. No matter how much these ministers defend their wealth, our adversary clearly uses their wealth to blaspheme the way of truth among those in the world. But not only that, for these ministers also cause many in the church to become offended. The apostle Paul made this comment, "Therefore, if food makes my brother stumble, I will never again eat meat, lest I make my brother stumble" (1 Corinthians 8:13).

The Lord's saints

Acts 16:14-15 "Now a certain woman named Lydia heard us. She was a seller of purple from the city of Thyatira, who worshiped God. The Lord opened her heart to heed the things spoken by Paul. (15) And when she and her household were baptized, she begged us, saying, "If you have judged me to be faithful to the Lord, come to my house and stay." So, she persuaded us."

New testament examples

And so, what about the Lord's saints? Although the Lord's saints are also expected to trust Him to supply all of their needs, they are not required as the Lord's ministers are, to forsake all to follow Him. We have already stated earlier, that God provides a home for each of His children, as part of their needs in this life. In the above passage of scripture, we see that Lydia had her own home, which she made available to Paul and his ministry team to stay in. We also see from this passage, that Lydia had her own business, which was evidently quite prosperous, as she was able to comfortably accommodate Paul and his entire ministry team, in her home.

> Romans 16:3-5 "Greet Priscilla and Aquila, my fellow workers in Christ Jesus, (4) who risked their own necks for my life, to whom not only I give thanks, but also all the churches of the Gentiles. (5) Likewise greet the church that is in their house. Greet my beloved Epaenetus, who is the firstfruits of Achaia to Christ."

The two saints, Priscilla and Aquila, mentioned by Paul in the above passage of scripture, proved to be a great blessing to Paul's ministry, and to the church in general. They too had their own business, which was tentmaking (Acts 18:3), and they provided Paul with employment, when he was planting the church in Corinth and was lacking in finances (Corinth was a city in the region of Achaia, which is where Paul had decided to preach the gospel without taking up offerings). Evidently their business was also prosperous, for they had homes in Corinth (Acts 18:3), Ephesus (1 Corinthians 16:19), and Rome, and they always opened their homes to be used as

New testament examples

a base to start churches, which is why Paul greeted the church that was in their house, in Rome.

> *Philemon 1:22 "But, meanwhile, also prepare a guest room for me, for I trust that through your prayers I shall be granted to you."*

In the above passage of scripture, the apostle Paul asked Philemon, who was a fellow believer, to prepare a guest room for Paul to stay in. The reason Paul asked him to do so, was because Paul had stayed with this believer on numerous occasions before. And so, we see that Philemon also owned his own home, which he also opened to the church to hold meetings in (Philemon 1:2). Philemon was also a relatively wealthy man, because he had sent one of his slaves (Onesimus), to minister to Paul while he was being held as a prisoner in Rome. Paul had since witnessed to Onesimus and gotten him saved, and thus sent him back to Philemon, no longer just a slave, but now a brother in the Lord, as well (Philemon 1:16). And so, from these examples in scripture, we can clearly see that many of the disciples of the Lord in the early church, owned their own homes, and that it was not uncommon for some to also have their own businesses.

> *Ephesians 6:5-8 "Bondservants, be obedient to those who are your masters according to the flesh, with fear and trembling, in sincerity of heart, as to Christ; (6) not with eyeservice, as men-pleasers, but as bondservants of Christ, doing the will of God from the heart, (7) with goodwill doing service, as to the Lord, and not to men, (8) knowing that whatever good anyone does, he will receive the same from the Lord, whether he is a slave or free."*

New testament examples

In Paul's day, slavery was an accepted part of society, and many of the Lord's saints were born-again, while in slavery. But even though slavery was an accepted norm in society, the apostle Paul did encourage those who were called while slaves, to obtain their freedom, if they had opportunity to be made free (1 Corinthians 7:21). Slaves were required to work for their owners, and in turn, it was expected of their owners, to take care of their slaves' physical needs. In the above passage of scripture, the Holy Spirit counselled His saints to serve their masters, as if they were serving the Lord. He said that in doing so, that the Lord would reward them accordingly. And so, even in their state of slavery, God would prosper them. You will recall that we saw earlier, how God prospered Joseph, when he was Potiphar's slave. In today's society, slavery is no longer an accepted norm, but what has become an accepted norm, is people working for companies, in an employee, employer relationship. And so, the same principal would apply to the Lord's saints, that are employees today. The Holy Spirit continues to counsel His saints to serve their employers, as if they were serving the Lord. And He continues to say, that in so doing, that the Lord will reward them accordingly.

James 2:5 "Listen, my beloved brethren: Has God not chosen the poor of this world to be rich in faith and heirs of the kingdom which He promised to those who love Him?"

We have seen so far, that many of the Lord's saints were called while in slavery, and it is common knowledge, that in James's day, slaves were the poor of society. And so, from the above passage of scripture, the Holy Spirit

New testament examples

through the apostle James, reveals to us that most of the Lord's saints were called while being slaves, for He says that God had chosen the poor of this world, which at that time, were mainly the slaves of society. This agrees with the gospel message, for our Lord Jesus said, that He had come to preach the gospel to the poor (Matthew 11:5). God has not changed, for He is the same yesterday, today and forever (Hebrews 13:8). And so, God still chooses the poor of this world to be rich in faith. That means that the vast majority of saints that are called today, will be employees, and not employers.

1 Thessalonians 4:10-12 "But we urge you, brethren, that you increase more and more; (11) that you also aspire to lead a quiet life, to mind your own business, and to work with your own hands, as we commanded you, (12) that you may walk properly toward those who are outside, and that you may lack nothing."

Ephesians 4:28 "Let him who stole steal no longer, but rather let him labour, working with his hands what is good, that he may have something to give him who has need."

Although the majority of the Lord's saints were called while slaves, there were those who were called as freemen, as well. In the above passages of scripture, the Holy Spirit counselled those who were free, to work with the own hands, so that they would not lack in anything, and that they would have an excess, so that they could bless others. And so, we see that those who were free in Paul's day, were encouraged by the Holy Spirit to find employment, so that God could meet their needs through

New testament examples

that employment. The Holy Spirit has not changed His counsel to the church, and still encourages His saints to work with their own hands, that they may lack nothing, and that they may have something to give to those in need.

> *Colossians 4:1 "Masters, give your bondservants what is just and fair, knowing that you also have a Master in heaven."*

As we saw in an earlier scripture, slavery was an accepted part of society in Paul's day, and many of the Lord's saints were born-again, while in slavery. But while many of the Lord's saints were born-again while in slavery, so there were some of His saints that were born-again, while owning slaves themselves. Again, because slavery was an accepted norm in society, the apostle Paul never admonished born-again slave owners, to set their slaves free, but rather he admonished them to treat their slaves justly and fairly, as evidenced in the above passage of scripture. And as we have already mentioned, the master and slave relationship in Paul's day, has been replaced with the employee, employer relationship that exists in companies today. And so, just as many of the Lord's saints today, are born-again as employees, so there are those who are born-again as employers. It is these saints, that the Holy Spirit continues to counsel to treat their employees, justly and fairly.

> *1 Timothy 6:17-19 "Command those who are rich in this present age not to be haughty, nor to trust in uncertain riches but in the living God, who gives us richly all things to enjoy. (18) Let them do good, that they be rich in good works, ready to give,*

New testament examples

willing to share, (19) storing up for themselves a good foundation for the time to come, that they may lay hold on eternal life."

As we saw earlier, most of the Lord's saints were called while slaves and in poverty, but there were also those who were called as freemen, who could work with their own hands. Nevertheless, not all were called while poor, for as revealed in the above passage of scripture, some were called while being rich, and we also saw earlier, that some of the Lord's disciples when He was on the earth, were very wealthy indeed.

1 Corinthians 1:26 "For you see your calling, brethren, that not many wise according to the flesh, not many mighty, not many noble, are called."

But even though there were some who were called while being rich, as the above passage of scripture reveals to us, there were not many saints that fell into this category. For you will recall that our Lord Jesus said, that it was hard for rich people to enter the kingdom of God, for they preferred to trust in their riches, rather than to trust in God (Mark 10:23-25). The attitude of the rich in our Lord's day, remains the same among the rich today, and so it is still not many rich, that enter the kingdom of God. Nevertheless, God does call some into His kingdom while they are rich, and it is these saints that need to rely on the grace of God, to keep them from becoming haughty and to keep them from trusting in uncertain riches, and to be rich in good works. And this God will do, for God knows what He is doing, and if He calls someone into His kingdom while they are rich, then He also gives them the grace to handle those riches in a godly manner. And so,

New testament examples

we see from the above examples, that the Lord's saints were brought into the kingdom from all walks of life, although most were brought in while in poverty. But clearly, we can see from the above examples, that God always counselled His saints in every walk of life, to follow godly lifestyles so that they could prosper and not lack anything. And even those who were rich, our Lord never encouraged to give up their riches, but rather to become rich in good works. And so, unlike the Lord's ministers, the Lord's saints have received no specific mandate in the area of finances, other than to live godly lifestyles.

Chapter 4
Walking in prosperity

The gospel to the poor

In this chapter, we will discuss certain principles taught in scripture, which if applied, will have the effect of blessing the saint so that they can walk in the full supply that our Lord Jesus has made available to us. But I need to make this statement up front. None of these principles will work for the believer, unless they are applied in faith. You have to believe that God's word is true, and that if acted upon, it will produce the results that God has promised, for the just shall live by faith, and we can receive nothing from God, except by faith. These principles can be applied as works, and they will be of no benefit to the believer, but for the Christian who applies them, by showing their faith by their works, they can fully expect to see the blessing of God being made manifest in their lives. We have already seen in an earlier section, that the vast majority of the Lord's saints, are poor when they are brought into the kingdom of God. However, it is not the Lord's will, that His saints stay that way, and in this section, we will look at how Jesus leads His saints out of poverty, into the place where they can walk in a full supply. Obviously, that which we learn in this section can be applied in the lives of all believers, not only in the lives of believers that are poor.

Luke 4:17-19 "And He was handed the book of the prophet Isaiah. And when He had opened the book, He found the place where it was written: (18)

Walking in prosperity

"The Spirit of the Lord is upon Me, because He has anointed Me to preach the gospel to the poor: He has sent Me to heal the broken-hearted, to proclaim liberty to the captives and recovery of sight to the blind, to set at liberty those who are oppressed; (19) To proclaim the acceptable year of the Lord."

Luke 7:22 "Jesus answered and said to them, "Go and tell John the things you have seen and heard: that the blind see, the lame walk, the lepers are cleansed, the deaf hear, the dead are raised, the poor have the gospel preached to them."

In the first passage of scripture quoted above, our Lord Jesus revealed to us, part of the mandate that He had received from God the Father. Essentially, He said that He was sent to heal the sick, set the captives free, and preach the gospel to the poor. In the second passage of scripture quoted above, our Lord confirmed to John the Baptist, that He was accomplishing that which the Father had sent Him to do, i.e. the sick were being healed, the dead were being raised, and the poor were hearing the gospel preached. In the gospel accounts, we can clearly see the results of the sick being healed, for all who came to Jesus believing, received their healing. And we see accounts of the dead being raised. But what about the poor? We know that Jesus frequently gave to the poor, but even though His ministry was extremely generous in giving to the poor, He did not have enough finances available, to deliver all the poor from their poverty. So how did Jesus minister to the poor, to deliver them from their poverty? The answer to that question, is that the scripture said that Jesus, "preached the gospel to them". In other words, Jesus taught them the principles of the

Walking in prosperity

kingdom of God, that if they applied to their lives, would deliver the poor from their poverty, and bring them into a place, where they could walk in an abundant supply.

Matthew 6:31-33 "Therefore do not worry, saying, 'What shall we eat?' or 'What shall we drink?' or 'What shall we wear?' (32) For after all these things the Gentiles seek. For your heavenly Father knows that you need all these things. (33) But seek first the kingdom of God and His righteousness, and all these things shall be added to you."

So, what were the principles that our Lord Jesus taught us to apply, so that we could walk free from poverty, and walk in an abundant supply? The first principle that our Lord taught us, is in the above quoted passage of scripture, i.e. we first need to become a part of the kingdom of God, for we need to seek first the kingdom of God and His righteousness. In other words, we must be born-again, and then as God's children, He will supply all of our needs. And so, we see that all believers meet this first condition that our Lord taught, to walking in a full supply. But clearly not all believers walk in a full supply, and so there must be further principles that need to be applied after we are born-again, if we are to walk in God's prosperity.

Mark 11:22-23 "So Jesus answered and said to them, "Have faith in God. (23) For assuredly, I say to you, whoever says to this mountain, 'Be removed and be cast into the sea,' and does not doubt in his heart, but believes that those things he says will be done, he will have whatever he says."

Walking in prosperity

The principle that our Lord Jesus taught on faith, in the above passage of scripture, is that we must speak to the mountain. Many believers never see results in their life, because they refuse to speak to the mountain, because they view it as foolishness. However, the apostle Paul said that spiritual things are foolishness to the natural man (1 Corinthians 2:14). And so, if you are going to prosper financially, then you are going to have to learn to speak God's word over your life. It is significant that in this one verse of scripture when Jesus taught on faith, that He used the word "say" three times, whereas He used the word "believe", only once. Most of the time, we as believers, put the emphasis on our believing. Whereas Jesus, in this passage of scripture, put the emphasis on our speaking. Don't misunderstand me, we must believe. But very often, our faith doesn't work for us, because we do not watch what we say. Jesus did not only teach us that we will have what we believe, He also taught us that we will have what we say. You must consistently speak what you believe in your heart, if you want to see it come to pass.

2 Corinthians 5:21 "For He made Him who knew no sin to be sin for us, that we might become the righteousness of God in Him."

We can receive nothing from God, except by faith (James 1:6-7). The above passage of scripture, plainly teaches us that as believers, we have been made the righteousness of God, in Christ Jesus. The reason God could do that for us, was because Jesus became sin, for us. In other words, Jesus took upon Himself our sin, so that we could take upon ourselves, His righteousness. And so, whether we believe it or not, the fact remains that when

Walking in prosperity

we were born-again, we became the righteousness of God in Christ Jesus. However, it is one thing to be made the righteous of God in Christ Jesus, but it is an entirely different thing, to walk in that righteousness. Only saints that truly believe that they have been made the righteousness of God in Christ Jesus, will ever walk in that righteousness. So how do we do that? The way that we were born-again, is that we believed in Jesus, and we confessed Him as Lord before men. When we did that, then God's power was released, and the miracle of the new birth took place in our spirits. And so, in the same manner, the saints that believe that God has made them righteous, and continually confess that they are righteous, will begin to walk in His righteousness. For it is through faith, that God's power is released in them, to enable them to walk in His righteousness. So, what does that principle have to do with having our needs met?

> *2 Corinthians 8:9 "For you know the grace of our Lord Jesus Christ, that though He was rich, yet for your sakes He became poor, that you through His poverty might become rich."*

We have already looked at one aspect of our redemption, i.e. how to walk in His righteousness. We saw that we can walk in His righteousness, because He was made to be sin for us. The above passage of scripture, uses the same language to describe what Christ did for us, in the area of walking free from poverty, and walking in abundant provision. For the scripture says that He became poor, that we through His poverty, might become rich. And so, just as with regards to our being made righteous, it is an accomplished fact that we have been made rich, through the poverty of Jesus, whether we

Walking in prosperity

choose to believe it or not. For those saints who choose to believe it however, they can begin to walk in the abundant provision that Jesus has made available to them, i.e. they can become rich. So how do we do that? We do it the same way as with every aspect of our Christian walk, we do it by faith, i.e. we must believe that we have been made rich through the poverty of Jesus, and we must also continually confess that we have been made rich through His poverty. It is when we do that, that the power of God is released in our lives, to cause us to walk in His abundant provision.

Faith requires action

There are certain promises in God's word, that when acted upon in faith, always produce instant results. For example, the miracle of the new birth, always happens the moment that the unsaved accept Christ Jesus as their Lord and Saviour, i.e. there is no delay and there is also no gradual transition from being spiritually dead, to being born-again. All are instantly born-again. And then there are some promises of God, that when acted upon, can produce instant results, but can also produce results over a period of time. Physical healing is an example of this type of promise, for there are times when hands are laid on an individual to receive healing, and they are instantly healed. But there are also times when hands are laid on an individual to receive healing, and although they begin to recover from that moment, their healing is progressive, and they only fully recover over a period of time. The promise of financial prosperity, falls into the category of being manifested over a period of time. The reason for that, is because in order for the believer to enjoy financial

Walking in prosperity

prosperity, God has to change the believer's lifestyle, and that takes time.

> *Romans 8:4-14 "that the righteous requirement of the law might be fulfilled in us who do not walk according to the flesh but according to the spirit. (5) For those who live according to the flesh set their minds on the things of the flesh, but those who live according to the spirit, the things of the spirit. ... (12) Therefore, brethren, we are debtors--not to the flesh, to live according to the flesh. (13) For if you live according to the flesh you will die; but if by the Spirit you put to death the deeds of the body, you will live. (14) For as many as are led by the Spirit of God, these are sons of God."*

When we walk in God's righteousness by faith, then two things begin to happen. We find that we no longer desire to walk in the flesh, for the flesh is against the righteousness of God. But rather we find that our desire is to walk in the spirit, for the spirit is life because of righteousness. In other words, our thinking begins to change. In the above passage of scripture, the Holy Spirit teaches us that those who walk in righteousness, no longer think as the flesh thinks, but rather as the spirit thinks, for He says that those who live according to the flesh set their minds on the things of the flesh, but those who live according to the spirit, the things of the spirit. The same passage of scripture, teaches us that it is the Holy Spirit that both enables us and leads us, to put to death the deeds of the body. And so, we see that in all of this, it is the Spirit of God that works in the believer, both to will and to do according to His good pleasure (Philippians 2:13). In the same manner, when we begin to

Walking in prosperity

walk in God's provision by faith, the Holy Spirit begins to lead us and also enable us, to start putting into practice, Godly principles in this area. In other words, our thinking begins to change, and thus our lifestyles begin to change, for the way we think determines the way we behave.

A balanced lifestyle

John 6:12 "So when they were filled, He said to His disciples, "Gather up the fragments that remain, so that nothing is lost."

There are three main areas that begin to change in our lives, when we begin to exercise our faith in God's provision for our lives. The first is that we start becoming more responsible, and less wasteful, in our handling of our finances. The above passage of scripture, gives us a bit of insight into our Lord's attitude regarding wastefulness. For when He fed the multitudes, He would not allow anything to go to waste. When God begins to change our attitudes, we too will have the same outlook on life that our Lord Jesus has, and we will cut back on wastefulness in our lives. You will be surprised just how much can be saved, when you look at your handling of finances in this manner.

1 Thessalonians 4:10-12 "But we urge you, brethren, that you increase more and more; (11) that you also aspire to lead a quiet life, to mind your own business, and to work with your own hands, as we commanded you, (12) that you may walk properly toward those who are outside, and that you may lack nothing."

Walking in prosperity

In the above passage of scripture, the Holy Spirit instructs the believer to aspire to lead a quiet life. One who leads a quiet life, is content with what they have, and is not striving to get more. The Holy Spirit goes on to say, that believers should work with their own hands, so that they may lack nothing. And so, when believers begin to apply themselves, in whatever work the Lord has given them to do, and they begin to live a quiet life, content with that which they have, they will very soon find that they will lack for nothing.

2 Thessalonians 3:10-12 "For even when we were with you, we commanded you this: If anyone will not work, neither shall he eat. (11) For we hear that there are some who walk among you in a disorderly manner, not working at all, but are busybodies. (12) Now those who are such we command and exhort through our Lord Jesus Christ that they work in quietness and eat their own bread."

The Holy Spirit cannot make it any plainer than that, i.e. if anyone will not work, neither shall he eat. Laziness is not condoned in the kingdom of God, and the scripture states that one who is slothful in their work, is a brother to him who is a great destroyer (Proverbs 18:9). When we begin to exercise our faith in God's prosperity for our lives, then we will find that we will begin to apply ourselves in our work that much more diligently, for the scripture says that, he who has a slack hand becomes poor, but the hand of the diligent makes rich (Proverbs 10:4). In the above passage of scripture, the Holy Spirit says that the believer who will not work, shall not eat. In other words, the church is instructed not to help those individuals. If God instructs the church not to help those

Walking in prosperity

individuals, then neither is God going to help them. However, the scripture does not say that those who "cannot" work, shall not eat, for there are those who have no employment, but are actively seeking employment. In those instances, the church must help those in need, and at the same time God will help them to find employment, as they put their trust in Him.

Ephesians 4:28 "Let him who stole steal no longer, but rather let him labour, working with his hands what is good, that he may have something to give him who has need."

In the above passage of scripture, the Holy Spirit again teaches us that as believers, we are to work with our own hands, and that when we do, we will find that we have excess to give to those in need. In all of the above scriptures, the Holy Spirit emphasizes to the believer, that they need to be working. God would not instruct His church to do something that they cannot do. And so, believers that do not have employment, can ask God to provide them with a job, and fully expect that God will do just that. For as we have seen, it is God's will that His children have employment, so that they can eat their own bread, lack nothing, and have excess to give to those who are in need.

1 Timothy 6:6-10 "Now godliness with contentment is great gain. (7) For we brought nothing into this world, and it is certain we can carry nothing out. (8) And having food and clothing, with these we shall be content. (9) But those who desire to be rich fall into temptation and a snare, and into many foolish and harmful lusts

Walking in prosperity

which drown men in destruction and perdition. (10) For the love of money is a root of all kinds of evil, for which some have strayed from the faith in their greediness and pierced themselves through with many sorrows."

We have already seen that the Holy Spirit encourages the believers to aspire to live quiet lives, and we said that one who leads a quiet life, will be content with what they have, and will not be striving to get more. The above passage of scripture, reinforces this truth to us, for the Holy Spirit teaches us that godliness with contentment is great gain. When believers begin to exercise their faith in God's prosperity, they will find that their level of contentment with what they have, will begin to rise, and their level of desire for that which they don't have, will begin to fall away. The reason that many believers get themselves into financial difficulties, is because they allow themselves to be tempted to want more than they need, i.e. they strive to gratify their fleshly desires. Nevertheless, when God's word begins to take effect in our lives, we find that half of what we thought we needed, we didn't need at all. And so, God brings a balance to our lives, where spiritual things become more important than material things. Now that doesn't mean that God no longer adds material blessings to our lives, for He does. It's just that, unlike those who strive after riches and so pierce themselves through with many sorrows, when God adds riches to us, He adds no sorrow with it (Proverbs 10:22).

Ephesians 6:5-8 "Bondservants, be obedient to those who are your masters according to the flesh, with fear and trembling, in sincerity of heart, as to

Walking in prosperity

Christ; (6) not with eyeservice, as men-pleasers, but as bondservants of Christ, doing the will of God from the heart, (7) with goodwill doing service, as to the Lord, and not to men, (8) knowing that whatever good anyone does, he will receive the same from the Lord, whether he is a slave or free."

1 Timothy 6:1-2 "Let as many bondservants as are under the yoke count their own masters worthy of all honour, so that the name of God and His doctrine may not be blasphemed. (2) And those who have believing masters, let them not despise them because they are brethren, but rather serve them because those who are benefited are believers and beloved. Teach and exhort these things."

On numerous occasions in the new testament, the Holy Spirit counsels the saints to apply themselves in their work, not with eyeservice, as men-pleasers, but as bondservants of Christ. I have quoted just two of those scriptures above, but there are many others. And so, we see that if we are going to experience the blessing of God in our work environment, then we must apply ourselves in our work, as those who work for the Lord. This is one of the areas where God changes our attitudes, for when we begin to apply ourselves in our work, as working for the Lord, then we will find that the quality of our work will become more excellent, and we will find that God enables us to become more productive. Through all of this, God is then able to give us favour with our employers, and we will find that promotions and above average salary increases start coming our way. You will recall that we saw earlier, how God gave Joseph favour with his employers, which resulted in him being promoted. But

Walking in prosperity

nevertheless, in all things we work as unto the Lord, and not to receive promotions and increases, for that we leave in the hands of the Lord. I want you to also notice, that the Lord admonishes us to serve both believing and unbelieving employers equally, for in both instances we are working for the Lord.

Ephesians 6:9 "And you, masters, do the same things to them, giving up threatening, knowing that your own Master also is in heaven, and there is no partiality with Him."

Colossians 4:1 "Masters, give your bondservants what is just and fair, knowing that you also have a Master in heaven."

Just as the Holy Spirit counsel's employees to do their work as unto the Lord, so He counsel's those who are employers, to treat their staff justly and fairly. For obviously, those who do so, can expect the Lord to bless them, by making their staff more productive. But again, just as with employees, employers are to do all things as unto the Lord, not to be blessed, for that we leave in the hands of the Lord.

Giving

2 Corinthians 9:6-11 "But this I say: He who sows sparingly will also reap sparingly, and he who sows bountifully will also reap bountifully. (7) So, let each one give as he purposes in his heart, not grudgingly or of necessity; for God loves a cheerful giver. (8) And God is able to make all grace abound toward you, that you, always having all sufficiency

Walking in prosperity

in all things, may have an abundance for every good work. (9) As it is written: "He has dispersed abroad, he has given to the poor; his righteousness endures forever. (10) Now may He who supplies seed to the sower, and bread for food, supply and multiply the seed you have sown and increase the fruits of your righteousness, (11) while you are enriched in everything for all liberality, which causes thanksgiving through us to God."

The second area that begins to change in our lives, when we begin to trust God to prosper us, is that we start to become more liberal in our giving. The above passage of scripture, is specifically referring to the giving of finances, for the Holy Spirit speaks of our having all sufficiency in all things and giving to the poor. There are two things that the Holy Spirit teaches us from this passage, that I want to highlight. Firstly, we can only reap that which we sow, and the amount we reap, is directly proportional to the amount we sow. And so, it is so important for believers to begin giving as soon as possible after they come into the kingdom of God, and to continue giving throughout their Christian walk in this life, so that they may enjoy a continual harvest. Someone said, but I can't afford to give. There are many in body of Christ, that are in dire financial need themselves, and so how do they begin to give? One way, would be to fast one meal a week for example, and use that money to pay for a meal for someone less fortunate than yourself, and that would be seed sown, which God can use to multiply, and give you a harvest. The point is, to start sowing where you are, and expect the Lord to give increase to your seed sown, for God always multiplies our seed sown. The second, and more important thing, that the Holy Spirit teaches us in

Walking in prosperity

the above passage, is that our attitude in giving, is very important to God, for God looks on the heart. There are two ways that believers can give. They can either give out of the flesh, or they can give out of the spirit. If they give out of the flesh, one or more of the following attitudes, will be made manifest. They will either give grudgingly, because they believe that it is expected of them to give. Or they will give from necessity, because they believe that if they don't give, then God won't bless them, and He may even allow a curse to come upon them. Or they will give from an attitude of pride, boasting to themselves and to God, because of how much they do give. None of these attitudes pleases God, and so if believers find that any one of these attitudes are motivating them to give, then they should rather refrain from giving, for God will not bless that, and they will not reap a harvest. Those who give from the spirit however, will always give from an attitude of love, i.e. love for God and love for others. And it is only when we give from an attitude of love, that we experience God's blessing, for the scripture teaches us, that even though we bestow all our goods to feed the poor, but have not love, it profits us nothing (1 Corinthians 13:3). The above scripture says, that we are to give as we purpose in our hearts. So, what does that mean? It simply means that the believer must want to give, i.e. their only motive for giving, is because they want to. Love gives, expecting nothing in return.

> *2 Corinthians 8:12-15 "For if there is first a willing mind, it is accepted according to what one has, and not according to what he does not have. (13) For I do not mean that others should be eased, and you burdened; (14) but by an equality, that now at this time your abundance may supply their lack,*

Walking in prosperity

that their abundance also may supply your lack-- that there may be equality. As it is written, "He who gathered much had nothing left over, and he who gathered little had no lack."

So how much should we give? In the previous passage of scripture, we saw that God supplies both our seed that we sow, and our bread for our food. Our bread for our food, refers to our needs being met. It is in this area, that Christians need to be careful that they are being led by the Spirit of God, for when God blesses us financially, the temptation can be very strong, to believe that we need more. What do I mean? For example, we may be living in a comfortable home where we are very happy, and then we get an increase in our income, and the temptation then arises for us to look for a bigger home in a more affluent area. And so, instead of the extra income that we have received, becoming part of our seed that we sow, it has now become part of our need, and our seed remains the same, or even diminishes. Even in the world, there are those who are extremely wealthy, and yet live rather moderate lifestyles, i.e. they live in comfortable homes and not in extravagant palatial homes, even though they can quite easily afford them. If those in the world, can live like that, how much more should believers not get caught up in the lust for things in this life. Do not misunderstand me, God gives us richly all things to enjoy (1 Timothy 6:17), but there is always a balance. You will recall the parable our Lord taught, about the rich man that received great increase, and built greater barns to store up his excess. Our Lord said that he was foolish, because he laid up treasures for himself, and was not rich toward God (Luke 12:21). Therefore, believers should always be led by the Spirit when it comes to determining

Walking in prosperity

what their needs are, for He has promised to supply all of our needs. And so, after our needs have been met, our seed is the excess that we have left over. In the above passage of scripture, the Holy Spirit confirms this truth, by telling the saints that they should give from their abundance, to supply the lack of others. It is from our abundance that we must learn to sow bountifully, for in doing so, we will reap bountifully. Notice that the scripture says, that He who gathered much had nothing left over. And so, it is scriptural to sow all of your seed, and not hang on to your seed, but there is always a balance, and we must be led by the Holy Spirit at all times.

2 Corinthians 9:9 "As it is written: "He has dispersed abroad, he has given to the poor; his righteousness endures forever."

Galatians 6:9-10 "And let us not grow weary while doing good, for in due season we shall reap if we do not lose heart. (10) Therefore, as we have opportunity, let us do good to all, especially to those who are of the household of faith."

So, who should we give to? We will have a look at the various areas where the saints should sow their seed, but ultimately the saint should be able to sow their seed into the local church and let the leadership of the church, administer those finances as good stewards, i.e. they should then apportion the finances received in the church correctly, being led by the Holy Spirit. An example in scripture, of a church operating in this area as God intended, is the church in Jerusalem, for the saints in that church, presented their offering to the apostles, who in

Walking in prosperity

turn distributed those finances, being led by the Holy Spirit (Acts 4:35). Scripture is very plain, regarding who we should give to, i.e. we are to give the poor, and more specifically, we are to give to the poor in the body of Christ. For we saw in the previous section, that our excess is meant to supply primarily, the lack of the saints. And so, the first category that the saints should give to, are the poor, and primarily the poor in the body of Christ. The above scriptures also confirm this truth for us, that we are to give to the poor, and especially to those who are of the household of faith. When the apostle Paul and his ministry team met with Peter, James and John, to compare the gospels that they were preaching, both teams came away from that meeting, not only agreeing on the gospel that each team was preaching, but also agreeing that they were to always remember the poor (Galatians 2:10). The apostle James, singles out widows and orphans among the poor, as being particularly vulnerable, and therefore deserving of the church's care (James 1:27).

> *1 Timothy 5:16 "If any believing man or woman has widows, let them relieve them, and do not let the church be burdened, that it may relieve those who are really widows."*

And so, all local churches, should have their own programs in place to assist the poor, particularly the poor in their own congregations. In the above passage of scripture, the apostle Paul reinforces this truth, by confirming that the church is meant to support the widows, that are in the church. You will recall that the church in Jerusalem, had a program in place that cared for the daily needs of their widows (Acts 6:1). And so, saints that attend churches that have such programs in

Walking in prosperity

place, should give into those programs. If, however, your local church does not have such a program in place, then the saints should look for other avenues to give to the poor, and not sow all of their seed into the local church.

1 Timothy 5:17-18 "Let the elders who rule well be counted worthy of double honour, especially those who labour in the word and doctrine. (18) For the Scripture says, "You shall not muzzle an ox while it treads out the grain," and, "The labourer is worthy of his wages."

Under the new covenant, the second category that the saints should give to, are the Lord's ministers of the gospel, and more specifically, those who are called to shepherd the local flock. In the above passage of scripture, the Holy Spirit is referring to the local pastors, when He states that the elders who rule well should be counted worthy of double honour. Normally, the local church leadership decides how much it gives to the local pastor, and so the saints are meant only to give into the church offerings. Obviously, the church leadership use these offerings for the operation of the church, as well. Nevertheless, saints should keep in mind that if their local church has no program in place that ministers to the poor, that part of the saints giving should be given to the poor, and not all to the church. The saints should be led by the Spirit, to determine how to apportion their giving between the two.

Philippians 4:15-18 "Now you Philippians know also that in the beginning of the gospel, when I departed from Macedonia, no church shared with me concerning giving and receiving but you only.

Walking in prosperity

(16) For even in Thessalonica you sent aid once and again for my necessities. (17) Not that I seek the gift, but I seek the fruit that abounds to your account. (18) Indeed, I have all and abound. I am full, having received from Epaphroditus the things sent from you, a sweet-smelling aroma, an acceptable sacrifice, well pleasing to God."

Then the third category that the saints should give to, are travelling ministries. There are ministry gifts, that the Lord uses to travel between churches, e.g. the apostle, the prophet and the evangelist. Normally these ministry gifts are supported financially, by the churches that fall within their sphere of influence. In the above passage of scripture, we see an example of the church at Philippi, sending financial support to the apostle Paul, while he was in Rome. But it also not uncommon in the body of Christ, for the Lord to impress upon certain members in His body, to financially support His travelling ministers. The saints Aquila and Priscilla, are two such examples, of saints that the Lord raised up, to support the apostle Paul's ministry (Romans 16:3-4). And so, saints that are led by the Lord to support travelling ministries, should also be led by the Spirit, to determine how to apportion their giving in this area.

Tithing

Malachi 3:8-11 "Will a man rob God? Yet you have robbed Me! But you say, 'In what way have we robbed You?' In tithes and offerings. (9) You are cursed with a curse, for you have robbed Me, Even this whole nation. (10) Bring all the tithes into the storehouse, that there may be food in My house, and

Walking in prosperity

try Me now in this," Says the Lord of hosts, "If I will not open for you the windows of heaven and pour out for you such blessing That there will not be room enough to receive it. (11) "And I will rebuke the devourer for your sakes, so that he will not destroy the fruit of your ground, nor shall the vine fail to bear fruit for you in the field," Says the Lord of hosts."

So, what about tithes? The above passage of scripture, is a favourite that is quoted, by those who would teach the church that she needs to tithe. There is one major problem with quoting this passage of scripture however, i.e. it is from the law, and the church is not under law. And so, if the Lord were to expect His church to observe this particular law, then He would also expect us to observe all of the law, for the scripture says that the man who does them, shall live by them (Galatians 3:12). But under the new covenant, the just shall live by faith (Galatians 3:11), and not by the law. Someone said, but tithing was introduced before the law of Moses, for both Abraham and Jacob tithed, and so that proves that tithing is not under the law. If the argument is put forward, that because tithing is mentioned in the bible before the law of Moses, that the church should practice it, then that same argument should apply for circumcision. For God also introduced circumcision through Abraham, long before the law of Moses, and yet in the new testament, the gentile believers are strongly warned against practicing circumcision (Galatians 5:2).

Genesis 14:18-20 "Then Melchizedek king of Salem brought out bread and wine; he was the priest of God Most High. (19) And he blessed him and

Walking in prosperity

said: "Blessed be Abram of God Most High, Possessor of heaven and earth; (20) And blessed be God Most High, Who has delivered your enemies into your hand." And he gave him a tithe of all."

Genesis 28:20-22 "Then Jacob made a vow, saying, "If God will be with me, and keep me in this way that I am going, and give me bread to eat and clothing to put on, (21) so that I come back to my father's house in peace, then the Lord shall be my God. (22) And this stone which I have set as a pillar shall be God's house, and of all that You give me I will surely give a tenth to You."

The above two passages, are the accounts recorded in scripture, of when Abraham gave his tithe to the Lord, and when Jacob committed to give his tithe to the Lord. In both accounts, both Abraham and Jacob decided of their own accord, to give one tenth to God. For at no time, did God instruct them to do so, but rather this was their own freewill offerings to the Lord. Under the law of Moses things changed however, for now God commanded the children of Israel to present their tithe before Him (Deuteronomy 14:22-29), and so tithing became a part of the law. There can be no doubt that the passage in Malachi is addressed to the children of Israel, who were under the law. It is interesting to note however, that even the Jews that are currently under the old covenant, no longer pay tithes. For under the law, God instructed them to pay their tithes to the Levitical priesthood, and in the current dispensation, that priesthood has been suspended. So, even though clearly, the passage in Malachi, is under the law, can it be applied to the church today? If the passage in Malachi is applicable to the

Walking in prosperity

church, it would mean that believers that do not tithe, are under a curse, for the scripture says, *"you are cursed with a curse, for you have robbed Me, even this whole nation"*. And yet under the new covenant, the scripture says that Christ has redeemed us from the curse of the law, having become a curse for us (Galatians 3:13). And for the passage in Malachi, to be applicable to the church, it would mean that only believers that tithe, can expect to be blessed financially, for the scripture says, *"I will open for you the windows of heaven and pour out for you such blessing that there will not be room enough to receive it"*. And yet under the new covenant, the scripture says that Christ has become poor, that we may become rich (2 Corinthians 8:9). And for the passage in Malachi, to be applicable to the church, it would mean that only believers that tithe, can expect to have the devourer rebuked, for the scripture says, *"I will rebuke the devourer for your sakes, so that he will not destroy the fruit of your ground, nor shall the vine fail to bear fruit for you in the field."* And yet under the new covenant, the scripture says that we are to resist the devil and he will flee from us (James 4:7), for greater is He that is in us than he that is in the world. The book of Malachi was written to the old covenant saints, who were not in Christ, and had no access to the blessing of the new covenant in Christ. And so, for the saints under the new covenant, to go before God and to expect Him to bless them, because they are observing the law under the old covenant, is foolishness. For in effect, they are saying to God, that their tithing carries more weight than that which Christ has already done for them. God will not honour that, for God will not violate the new covenant, which is in His Son.

Walking in prosperity

Galatians 4:21-26 "Tell me, you who desire to be under the law, do you not hear the law? (22) For it is written that Abraham had two sons: the one by a bondwoman, the other by a freewoman. (23) But he who was of the bondwoman was born according to the flesh, and he of the freewoman through promise, (24) which things are symbolic. For these are the two covenants: the one from Mount Sinai which gives birth to bondage, which is Hagar-- (25) for this Hagar is Mount Sinai in Arabia, and corresponds to Jerusalem which now is, and is in bondage with her children-- (26) but the Jerusalem above is free, which is the mother of us all."

Tithing, as all the law does, produces bondage. In the above passage of scripture, the apostle Paul warns the churches in Galatia about this fact, for he says that Christians who desire to be under the law, will subject themselves to the same bondage that the Jews are currently under. I have seen baby believers being placed under bondage financially, because they have been taught that they must tithe, and so they try give beyond their ability, and land up in financial trouble. I have also seen other believers being placed under bondage of condemnation, because they cannot afford to tithe. Anything that produces bondage, is not the new covenant, for we have been called to liberty (Galatians 5:13). The message of tithing is very manipulative, because it promises blessing to the one who practices it, while it warns of the withholding of blessing and pronounces a curse, on the one who does not practice it. Most believers want to be blessed and avoid being cursed, and so they will comply with that message. But the truth of the matter, is that all believers have already been blessed with every

Walking in prosperity

spiritual blessing in Christ (Ephesians 1:3), and all have already been redeemed from the curse of the law. The ones that really benefit from the message on tithing, are those who teach it, for that message assures them of a steady income, from the believers who have been placed under the bondage of that law. And so, because it is such a lucrative message to preach, there are many that take advantage of the ignorance of believers and continue to teach it. In fact, some of them place an even greater burden on the church, by telling them that they not only have to tithe, but they also have to give offerings over and above their tithe, thus pressurizing believers to give even more. Nevertheless, there are many genuine preachers that teach the church to tithe, not because they want to manipulate the church, but because they themselves are ignorant about the truth of the gospel, in this area. And those same genuine preachers, also practice tithing themselves, and they will testify that God has blessed them because they tithe. You will find in most cases however, that those preachers actually give far more than ten percent of their income, and so God blesses them for their giving, and not for their "tithing". In other words, God recognizes their ignorance, and blesses them in spite of it, but nevertheless, God does not take kindly to those preachers who try to manipulate His church in this area, and they will have to give an account for their actions. There are many examples in scripture, of those whom the Lord blessed, who never tithed. Job would be one such example. God blesses our giving, not our tithing. He who sows sparingly will reap sparingly, while he who sows bountifully will reap bountifully, i.e. the one who sows one percent of their income, will reap less than the one who sows twenty percent of their income, nevertheless, both will still reap a harvest. Ten percent is not some magic

Walking in prosperity

number, that if reached, only then releases the blessing of God in our lives.

> *Hebrews 7:4-10 "Now consider how great this man was, to whom even the patriarch Abraham gave a tenth of the spoils. (5) And indeed those who are of the sons of Levi, who receive the priesthood, have a commandment to receive tithes from the people according to the law, that is, from their brethren, though they have come from the loins of Abraham; (6) but he whose genealogy is not derived from them received tithes from Abraham and blessed him who had the promises. (7) Now beyond all contradiction the lesser is blessed by the better. (8) Here mortal men receive tithes, but there he, of whom it is witnessed that he lives. (9) Even Levi, who receives tithes, paid tithes through Abraham, so to speak, (10) for he was still in the loins of his father when Melchizedek met him."*

So, if tithing is not for the church, why did the writer mention it in the book of Hebrews? It is significant that the Holy Spirit mentions the subject of tithing, in the one letter in the new testament, that was specifically addressed to Jewish believers. In context, the Holy Spirit was teaching them the difference between the priesthood of Aaron, and the priesthood of Melchizedek. Our Lord Jesus is the high priest after the order of Melchizedek, and in the above passage, the scripture says in verse eight, that He received the tithes in heaven, while at the same time, the Levitical priests received the tithes here on earth. In other words, when the Jews under the old covenant, presented their tithes and offerings at the temple, those tithes and offerings were also received in heaven, which is

Walking in prosperity

entirely correct, for it was God that gave them their covenant. The same principle applies to the saints under the new covenant, for all of our giving is received both by men here on earth, and at the same time is received by our High Priest in heaven. Nevertheless, under the new covenant, it is entirely scriptural for Jewish believers to observe the law of Moses (Acts 21:20). Even the apostle Paul kept the law, for he said that, to the Jews he became as a Jew, that he might win Jews; and to those who were under the law, as under the law, that he might win those who were under the law (1 Corinthians 9:20). You will recall the account of Paul hastening to Jerusalem, so that he could be in time to keep the feast of tabernacles (Acts 18:21). And so, as Jewish believers, the Hebrew church, who still went to the temple daily to pray, also paid their tithes to the Levitical priesthood. God recognized that, as part of their freewill offerings to Him, which is why Jesus received their tithes. But the Holy Spirit counsels the gentile believers not to attempt observing the law (Galatians 3:2-13), for that is not how God called us into His kingdom. And so, just as gentile believers are instructed not to observe days, months, seasons and years (Galatians 4;10), neither are we to observe tithing. But rather, as gentile believers, we are to give from our abundance, which may initially be a small amount, but as God gives us increase, that amount will steadily grow, and eventually the believer will find that they are giving far more, than merely a tenth of their income.

Creating wealth

Deuteronomy 8:18 "And you shall remember the Lord your God, for it is He who gives you power

Walking in prosperity

to get wealth, that He may establish His covenant which He swore to your fathers, as it is this day."

The third area that begins to change in our lives when we start believing God to prosper us, is that we start becoming more industrious, in the ways we earn money. The above passage of scripture, is a promise that God gave to the children of Israel. In that promise, God said that He would give the children of Israel, power to get wealth. A more accurate translation of that passage, would be that God had promised to give them, the ability to create wealth. That same promise is available to the sons of God today. You will recall that we looked at the example earlier, of the idea that God gave to Jacob, as to how to increase his livestock. When believers begin to exercise their faith in securing the riches that Jesus has provided for us, they will begin to find for example, that ideas and opportunities will come their way, on how to generate extra income streams.

Isaiah 48:17 "Thus says the Lord, your Redeemer, The Holy One of Israel: "I am the Lord your God, Who teaches you to profit, Who leads you by the way you should go."

God is a God of increase, and He delights in the prosperity of His children, for God is not opposed to His children being rich, He is opposed to His children being covetous. In the scripture quoted above, God tells us, that it is He who teaches us how to profit. In context, this passage is speaking about both spiritual and financial prosperity. When God says that He leads us in the way we should go, He is referring to His teaching us how to profit. And so, we see that if we will learn to follow the Lord's

Walking in prosperity

leading in life, that He in fact teaches us just how to become rich. Believers who exercise their faith in this area, will find for example, that God will show them where to get the best deal when they need to purchase something. God will begin to show them a number of different ways, in which they can cut back on their expenses, and increase their income, thus increasing their overall profit.

> *John 14:26 "But the Helper, the Holy Spirit, whom the Father will send in My name, He will teach you all things, and bring to your remembrance all things that I said to you."*

In the above passage of scripture, our Lord Jesus said that when the Holy Spirit comes, He will teach us all things. Every born-again believer has the Holy Spirit residing on the inside of them, and He has been sent by the Lord, to teach us all things. All things mean all things, and so that includes how to profit, or to become rich. We have already seen in this teaching, that it is the will of the Lord that His children become rich, and so the Holy Spirit has no problem with teaching us just how to do that. But you will recall that our Lord Jesus also taught us, that in order for us to receive from God, that we must first ask (Luke 11:10). The reason that many believers never learn how to become rich, is because they never ask God to show them how to profit. And so, we must ask. But we must ask in faith, for our Lord Jesus also taught us that it is whatever we ask in prayer, believing, that we will receive (Matthew 21:22). Once you have asked in faith, then expect God to begin to show you how to profit in your finances, and that is exactly what He will do.

Walking in prosperity

Divine favour

2 Corinthians 9:8-11 *"And God is able to make all grace abound toward you, that you, always having all sufficiency in all things, may have an abundance for every good work. (9) As it is written: " He has dispersed abroad, he has given to the poor; his righteousness endures forever." (10) Now may He who supplies seed to the sower, and bread for food, supply and multiply the seed you have sown and increase the fruits of your righteousness, (11) while you are enriched in everything for all liberality, which causes thanksgiving through us to God."*

And then finally, when we begin to exercise our faith in God's provision, we will find that God begins to intervene miraculously in our lives, by giving us supernatural favour. The above passage of scripture, says that God is able to make all grace abound toward us. Part of what that means, is that supernatural blessing will be bestowed upon us. For example, unexpected promotions at work will come our way. New job opportunities will be made available to us. New business opportunities will come our way. The list is endless, for with God nothing is too hard, and nothing is impossible. My experience in this area, is that these blessings come completely, "out of the blue", so to speak. When we least expect it, then God manifests His grace in our lives, and all we can do is give Him thanks for His abundant grace, for He truly is a good God.

Chapter 5
Our adversary

There is only one thief

    John 10:10 "The thief does not come except to steal, and to kill, and to destroy. I have come that they may have life, and that they may have it more abundantly."

    There is only one person that tries to steal from us, and who tries to kill and destroy us, and his name is Satan. God on the other hand, is for us, and He has proven this, by sending His Son Jesus Christ, to bless us with life more abundantly. In the above passage of scripture, our Lord Jesus plainly revealed this truth to us. And so, when believers have material possessions stolen from them, the one who is behind that theft is the thief himself, Satan. When believers have sicknesses and diseases that attack their physical bodies, thus robbing them of their health and their finances, which are used to pay for medical treatment, then the one who is behind that sickness, is the one who always tries to kill, Satan. And when believers have incidents occurring in their lives that are destructive, such as motor vehicle accidents for example, then the one behind those incidents, is the destroyer himself, Satan. Now as we will see in this section, Satan cannot do just as he pleases in the life of the believer, for there is always a cause, that allows Satan to gain access to the lives of believers, but nevertheless, the fact remains, that all incidents of theft and destruction,

Our adversary

that take place in the lives of believers, are orchestrated by our adversary the devil.

Our hedge

> Job 1:9-10 *"So Satan answered the Lord and said, "Does Job fear God for nothing? (10) Have You not made a hedge around him, around his household, and around all that he has on every side? You have blessed the work of his hands, and his possessions have increased in the land."*

There are a number of truths that are revealed to us in the above passage of scripture. Now I know that Satan is the one who is doing the talking in this passage, but he is talking to the Lord, and so everything that he is saying is factual, and not a lie. Firstly, we see that it is God who blesses us, but I want you to notice what it is that God blesses, for the scripture says that He blesses the work of our hands. And so, we again see how important it is, that whatever our hands find to do, that we do it with all our might (Ecclesiastes 9:10). Secondly, we see that when the Lord blesses the work of our hands, that the result is, that our possessions begin to increase. In other words, we will start becoming richer. And then we get to third truth revealed in this passage, which is the part that affects our adversary the devil, and that is the hedge that God places around us. I want you to notice the three areas that God placed a hedge around. For the scripture tells us, that God placed a hedge around Job, around Job's household, and God also placed a hedge around all that Job owned. As we discuss this section in more detail, we will see that it is important for believers to place a hedge around all three areas, and not just one or two. As a result of the hedges

Our adversary

that God had placed around Job, his household, and all that he owned, Satan had no way in. It was in that state, that Job enjoyed the blessing of God in his life, for nothing was stolen from him, no sickness was present, and he experienced no incidents of destruction. That is the state that God wants each of His children to live in, for it was only when the hedges were removed from Job, that Satan was able to bring sickness and destruction into Job's life. Someone said, but I thought we were meant to suffer, and go through tribulations. That is correct, for that is what the bible teaches, but the bible is very clear as to which type of tribulation we are appointed to, i.e. we are meant to suffer as Christians (1 Peter 4:16). And so, Christian suffering can include being reviled and ostracised by men, having property confiscated, and even martyrdom, but all of that suffering is because we belong to Christ. We are not meant to suffer with sickness, poverty and incidents of destruction occurring in our lives, for that is the suffering that those in the world are subjected to, because they fall under the control of the god of this world, Satan (1 John 5:19), the one who kills, steals and destroys. In all things, we should always look at our Lord Jesus as our ultimate example, for the scripture says that we should walk even as He walked (1 John 2:6). Jesus was never sick, and we have seen earlier that Jesus always had His needs met. Something else that never happened to Jesus, is that He never experienced any form of accidents in His life. You will recall that the devil quoted the scripture to our Lord, when he tried to tempt Him in the wilderness, "If You are the Son of God, throw Yourself down. For it is written: 'He shall give His angels charge over You,' and, in their hands they shall bear you up, lest you dash your foot against a stone.'" (Matthew 4:6). That is exactly how Jesus walked this earth, i.e. He never even

Our adversary

once dashed His foot against a stone, for God had given His angels charge over His Son, to bear Him up in their hands. God is no respecter of persons, and what He did for His Firstborn Son, He will also do for the rest of His sons who are in Christ.

John 14:30 "I will no longer talk much with you, for the ruler of this world is coming, and he has nothing in Me."

In the above passage of scripture, our Lord stated that Satan had nothing in Him. In other words, Satan couldn't get to Jesus, because just like Job, God had placed a hedge around His Son. So how do we get to the place, where we too can walk where Satan cannot get to us?

1 John 5:18 "We know that whoever is born of God does not sin; but he who has been born of God keeps himself, and the wicked one does not touch him."

In the above passage of scripture, the Holy Spirit through the apostle John, teaches us how to walk in that place, where our adversary cannot get in. The first step, is that we are to stay away from sin, for He tells us that whoever is born of God, does not sin. Satan knows that sin opens the door to him, and so he will always try tempting the believer to commit sin. That's exactly what he did to Jesus, and so we are no different. But the same passage teaches us, that he who is born of God, keeps himself. The word translated "keep" can also be translated "to guard". In other words, believers that guard themselves, and stay away from temptation so that they do not walk in sin,

Our adversary

keep the door closed on Satan. For the scripture says that the wicked one does not touch them. That means that Satan cannot put sickness on their bodies, he cannot steal from them, and he cannot bring destruction into their lives.

>*Ephesians 4:26-27 "Be angry, but do not sin": do not let the sun go down on your wrath, (27) nor give place to the devil."*

In the above passage of scripture, the Holy Spirit through the apostle Paul, again reinforces the truth that sin opens the door to Satan, for He tells us that believers who do not sin, do not give any place to the devil. And so, we can clearly see that if we want to walk in that place where our adversary cannot touch us, then we must walk free from sin. Someone said, but I thought it was impossible to walk free from sin. That's not what the new testament teaches us, for the new testament teaches us, that we have died to sin and so we no longer need to walk in it (Romans 6:2). (See my book, "Born Free from Sin", for more detail on this subject).

Our authority

>*Psalms 91:1-12 "He who dwells in the secret place of the Most High Shall abide under the shadow of the Almighty. (2) I will say of the Lord, "He is my refuge and my fortress; My God, in Him I will trust." ... (10) No evil shall befall you, nor shall any plague come near your dwelling; (11) For He shall give His angels charge over you, to keep you in all your ways. (12) In their hands they shall bear you up, lest you dash your foot against a stone."*

Our adversary

The above quoted Psalm, is used by many believers, to claim the Lord's protection for their lives. I have not quoted all of that Psalm, as that falls outside the scope of this teaching, nevertheless there are two points that I want to bring out from the above passage. Firstly, we saw earlier, that Satan himself quoted this Psalm to our Lord Jesus, when he was tempting Him in the wilderness, for he said, it is written: 'He shall give His angels charge over You,' and, in their hands they shall bear you up, lest you dash your foot against a stone.' " (Matthew 4:6). In other words, Satan understood that this Psalm was actually speaking about God's protection provided to Jesus, as the Son of God. But the second thing I want you to notice, is that God's protection was not automatically afforded to Jesus, because He was the Son of God. For the scripture says that Jesus confessed this Psalm over His life, for the scripture quoted Jesus as saying, "I will say of the Lord, "He is my refuge and my fortress; My God, in Him I will trust." In other words, Jesus confessed this Psalm over His life in faith, and as a result, that is what He experienced in His life. We are no different. If the Lord Jesus enjoyed the benefits of this Psalm, by confessing it over His life, then we must follow His example. Psalm ninety-one is not the only scripture that can be used in this manner, for there are many others. But the point that I wanted to make, is that the hedge that God places around His children is not automatic, we have to claim it by faith, by confessing it over our lives and the lives of our households, even as our Lord Jesus did. Someone said, but I thought that walking free from sin, keeps the door closed on Satan, and he cannot then affect our lives. The answer to that comment, is that we must do both, i.e. we must walk free from sin, thus not allowing Satan access to

Our adversary

our lives, and we must in faith, claim God's protection over our lives. You say, how do you know that we should do both? By looking at Jesus, the author and perfecter of our faith, for even though Jesus never once committed any sin, He still confessed Psalm ninety-one over His life.

1 Peter 5:8-9 "Be sober, be vigilant; because your adversary the devil walks about like a roaring lion, seeking whom he may devour. (9) Resist him, steadfast in the faith, knowing that the same sufferings are experienced by your brotherhood in the world."

So, does it mean that if we walk free from sin, and we confess God's promises of protection over our lives, that we will never have any problems with the devil? The answer to that question is a resounding, "no". Although as believers, we are not of this world, we are still living in this world, and the god of this world is Satan (2 Corinthians 4:4). And so, we live in a hostile environment, for the god of this world hates believers, and his purpose is only to kill, steal and destroy. The above passage of scripture, refers to him as our adversary, and as such, he is always looking for ways to gain access to our lives. But the same passage of scripture, tells us how to deal with him, for the Holy Spirit tells the believer to resist him, steadfast in the faith. So, what does that mean? What it means, is that there are going to be days when our adversary the devil, is going to bring circumstances into our lives, that are going to test our faith. The apostle Paul refers to it, as standing against the wiles of the devil, in the evil day (Ephesians 6:11-13).

Our adversary

Matthew 28:18-19 "And Jesus came and spoke to them, saying, "All authority has been given to Me in heaven and on earth. (19) Go therefore and make disciples of all the nations, baptizing them in the name of the Father and of the Son and of the Holy Spirit."

Ephesians 1:22-23 "And He put all things under His feet and gave Him to be head over all things to the church, (23) which is His body, the fullness of Him who fills all in all."

And so, we resist the devil, by exercising our authority over him. In the above two passages of scripture, we see the authority that has been delivered to the church, in the earth. In the first passage quoted, our Lord Jesus told us that all authority in heaven and in the earth, has been given to Him. When He said that, He then immediately delegated His authority in the earth, to His church, for He said, "Go therefore". In other words, we are to go into the earth, using His authority. In the second passage, we see that God has made Jesus head over all things, to the church. And so, again we see that the church (which is the body of Christ), has all things placed under her, which includes our adversary the devil.

Mark 4:37-39 "And a great windstorm arose, and the waves beat into the boat, so that it was already filling. (38) But He was in the stern, asleep on a pillow. And they awoke Him and said to Him, "Teacher, do You not care that we are perishing?" (39) Then He arose and rebuked the wind, and said to the sea, "Peace, be still!" And the wind ceased and there was a great calm."

Our adversary

All through this teaching, we have said that we must look at Jesus as our example. In the above passage of scripture, we have the account of the storm that arose, while Jesus and His disciples were crossing the sea of Galilee. There can be no doubt, that Satan was the one causing the storm, that threatened to sink the boat that Jesus and His disciples were sailing in. When Jesus was made aware of the situation, He arose and rebuked the wind and the sea. Ultimately, Jesus was rebuking Satan's angels, that had caused the storm in the first place. When Jesus did that, everything returned to normal.

Acts 16:16-18 "Now it happened, as we went to prayer, that a certain slave girl possessed with a spirit of divination met us, who brought her masters much profit by fortune-telling. (17) This girl followed Paul and us, and cried out, saying, "These men are the servants of the Most High God, who proclaim to us the way of salvation." (18) And this she did for many days. But Paul, greatly annoyed, turned and said to the spirit, "I command you in the name of Jesus Christ to come out of her." And he came out that very hour."

The above passage of scripture, is very enlightening for us, regarding the authority that believers have in the earth. Just like the rest of us, the apostle Paul grew in his understanding of how to walk this Christian walk, and this incident reveals that truth to us. The background to this incident, is that Paul and his ministry team had come to the city of Philippi to preach the gospel. As can we see from the above account, when Paul and his team went to prayer, a slave girl would wait for them and follow them,

Our adversary

proclaiming loudly to all who could hear, that Paul and his team were servants of the Most High God, who proclaimed the way of salvation. Everyone in town knew that this girl was a fortune-teller, and so it was not a good testimony for the Lord's ministers, to have the demon that had possessed her, acting as if he was a part of what they were doing. The scripture says that she did this for many days. So why did Paul tolerate this demon's behaviour for so long? The answer, is that Paul did not know that he could do something about it. Someone said, but Paul knew that as believers, we can cast out demons. It is one thing to cast demons out of people, that come to believers for deliverance, but it is something else entirely to go looking for people that are demon possessed, to cast out those demons. It may be that the person who is demon possessed want's that demon, and so for believers to try cast it out would be foolishness, for the demon won't go, as they have permission to stay in that house. But the above scenario was different, for the demon had initiated the intrusion into Paul's affairs, not the other way around. And so, eventually out of frustration, Paul commanded the demon to come out of her, and the demon came out that same hour. Had Paul known that he could do that, he would have done it the very first day, and not waited so long. Paul learnt something that day, and so do we, i.e. we have authority over Satan's realm if they ever try to hinder us in any way, and it is up to us to use that authority.

James 4:7 "Therefore submit to God. Resist the devil and he will flee from you."

And so, if we will learn to follow the examples given to us by our Lord Jesus and the apostle Paul, and rebuke the devil and his circumstances that he will try to bring

Our adversary

against us, we will experience the same results that Jesus and Paul did. For the scripture tells us as believers, to resist the devil and he will flee from us. In fact, there is no place in the new testament, where the church is taught to ask God to deal with the devil, but rather in all instances, the church is taught to deal with the devil ourselves, using the authority given to us in Jesus.

Malachi 3:11 "And I will rebuke the devourer for your sakes, so that he will not destroy the fruit of your ground, nor shall the vine fail to bear fruit for you in the field," Says the Lord of hosts."

There is one last comment that I want to make about our adversary, which is based on the deception of tithing. In the above passage of scripture, God promised the Jews that tithed, that He would rebuke the devourer for their sakes. God did that under the old covenant, because the Jews had no authority to rebuke Satan for themselves. It is only the saints under the new covenant, that have been given authority over all the power of the enemy (Luke 10:19). And so, because God has already given us all the authority we need to rebuke the devourer ourselves, He expects us to walk in that authority, and He no longer rebukes the devourer for our sakes. Satan knows that, and so he encourages the saints to claim the old covenant promise, of God rebuking him, for he knows that God will not do it, for God will not violate His new covenant. And so, you find many saints under the new covenant, tithing, and claiming the promise from God under the old covenant, to rebuke the devourer for their sakes, and nothing happens, but rather, the devourer continues to steal from them unabated. As sons of God,

Our adversary

we must walk in the light of the new covenant, and we will not be deceived.

If you believe you can receive Jesus as your Lord and Saviour by praying this prayer

Dear Heavenly Father,

I come to You in the Name of Jesus.

Your Word says, "the one who comes to Me I will by no means cast out" (John 6:37), so I know You won't cast me out, but You take me in and I thank You for it. You said in Your Word, "Whoever calls on the name of the lord shall be saved." (Romans 10:13). I am calling on Your Name, so I know that You save me right now. You also said, "If you confess with your mouth the Lord Jesus and believe in your heart that God has raised Him from the dead, you will be saved. (10) For with the heart one believes unto righteousness, and with the mouth confession is made unto salvation" (Romans 10:9-10). I believe in my heart Jesus Christ is the Son of God. I believe that He was raised from the dead for my justification, and I confess Him now as my Lord. Because Your Word says, "with the heart one believes unto righteousness," and I do believe with my heart, I have now become the righteousness of God in Christ Jesus (2 Cor. 5:21) . . .

And I am now saved!

Thank You, Lord!

Welcome to the family of God. Now that you are His child you need to read your bible (especially the New

Testament) daily, spend time in prayer daily and join a local church that will teach you to be filled with the Holy Spirit with the evidence of speaking in other tongues, so that you can grow spiritually. You also need to tell others how Jesus has saved you so that they too can be saved.

About the Author

From childhood, Michael E.B. Maher has always known that the Lord's call was upon his life for the ministry. When he was saved at the age of twenty-two, almost immediately the Lord Jesus began to deal with him about entering the ministry. He went to Oral Roberts University to enrol but circumstances prevented him from following that path. After a period, the call for the ministry once again became very strong, and finally in the early 1990's Michael entered the ministry. After a period, he left the ministry and went into the business world. Although he experienced success in the business world, he was outside of the Lord's will for his life. Over time, he began to drift from the close relationship with the Lord that he had always known. By 2010 the Lord's patience had run out, and Michael suffered his first series of heart attacks. By this time, Michael had become so worldly in his thinking that it never even occurred to him that the Lord had begun to judge him for his disobedience. After his medical treatment, Michael went back into his career thinking that all was back on track again. But now the Lord started to unravel his career as well. Whereas before he had always excelled in his work, he now found completely dissatisfied with what he was doing. And so, at the height of his career he decided to take early retirement. It was during this time that his relationship with the Lord grew again. Although the Lord had brought him to this point, he was still not in the Lord's will. And so, Michael then had his next series of heart attacks. It was only now that the Lord finally got his attention and he committed to the Lord that if He would spare his life, that he would finally answer the Lord's call to the ministry.

And so, in 2014 Michael Maher Ministries was begun. From the beginning, the mandate given to Michael from the Lord Jesus was to preach the word. And so, this ministry preaches the word of God on every available platform around the world.

Michael Maher Ministries

Free Subscription

Join hundreds of others from countries around the world and read our Daily Bible Teaching Email and more, that will help you to grow in your walk with the Lord Jesus.

Thank you, sir, for helping me to understand these teachings clearly! Amen

- *Tawanda Masvina*

Amen to keeping on keeping on. Thank you for today's lesson. We must never forget to pray regularly and immerse ourselves in the Word – "a page (or Chapter) a day helps keep Satan at bay".
Blessings,

- *John Lombard*

Thank you so much for today's inspiration. This made so much sense to me and helped me overcome a huge block in my understanding.
Blessings and love

- *Pam Laughton*

Log on to our website to subscribe.

www.mebmm.org

Michael Maher Ministries

Online Bible Courses

Our courses are designed to help believers grow in their faith and reach their full potential in Christ that God intended for their lives, through the study of His word.

Flexible

Enrol any time: choose your topic of study; study at your own pace.

Affordable

Pay as you go.

Log on to our website to register.

www.mebmm.org

Michael Maher Ministries

13 Windsor Lodge
Beach Road
Fish Hoek, 7974
Cape Town
South Africa
Phone: +27 082-974-3599

On the Web

www.mebmm.org

www.ingramcontent.com/pod-product-compliance
Lightning Source LLC
LaVergne TN
LVHW011721060526
838200LV00051B/2988